THE PRAYER

~ OF ~

THE FAITHFUL

SUSAN SAYERS

kevin
mayhew

kevin mayhew

First published in Great Britain in 2000 by Kevin Mayhew Ltd
Buxhall, Stowmarket, Suffolk IP14 3BW
Tel: +44 (0) 1449 737978 Fax: +44 (0) 1449 737834
E-mail: info@kevinmayhewltd.com

www.kevinmayhew.com

9 8 7 6 5 4 3 2 1 0

ISBN 978 1 84003 505 6
Catalogue No. 1500336

Cover design by Jonathan Stroulger
Edited by Katherine Laidler
Typeset by Louise Selfe

Printed and bound in Great Britain

FOREWORD

A praying church is a living organism, powered by the love of God, and directed by his will. The aim of those leading intercessions in public worship is to provide a suitable climate for prayer, both for the faithful core of praying members, and also for those who drift in as visitors, sometimes willingly and sometimes rather grudgingly.

Since our God is in a far better position to know the needs of each muddle of people who arrive on any particular Sunday, it is obviously sensible to prepare for leading the intercessions by praying for those who will be there, asking our God to lead us with his agenda in mind, rather than taking immediate charge ourselves. Then we have to give him a chance to answer! You may find that a quiet walk enables you to do this, or a time wandering round the empty church, or time spent on some of the mechanical jobs at home while you still your heart and resist the temptation to badger God with good ideas.

The ideas provided reflect the day's readings, and as you read through them you may well find that these ideas will spark off other thoughts of your own. Do use them however you wish – exactly as they stand, adapted to suit specific needs, or simply as a starting point. They are a resource to help you, not a cage to keep your own ideas out.

During the service be alert to what is being said and how God is moving among you, so that you can pick up on these threads, if it seems appropriate, during the intercessions. And if you have young children present, give some thought to how they can also be praying at this time. They might be following a picture prayer trail, singing a quiet worship song, drawing some situation they are praying for, or looking through the intercession pictures provided in children's communion books.

I have heard it said that since God can hear the prayers, it doesn't really matter if the congregation can't. I don't agree. In public worship it can be very distracting to be straining to hear, or isolating if you can hear only a vague mumble. Do take the trouble to practise speaking clearly and fairly slowly in the church, so that everyone can comfortably take in what you are saying. Bear in mind that nerves usually make us speed up somewhat, so speak extra slowly to allow for this.

Finally, don't recite what you have written, but pray it. Pray it both through the intentions and through the silences. Leading the intercessions carries a great responsibility, but it is also a great privilege.

SUSAN SAYERS
with Father Andrew Moore

CONTENTS

Year A

ORDINARY TIME

Year B

ADVENT

Year C

YEAR A

FIRST SUNDAY OF ADVENT

We are to wake up and make sure we stay ready for the second coming.

Celebrant
Let us pray to the God of all time and space,
in whose love we exist
and by whose love we are saved.

Reader
As we prepare ourselves
for the time when Christ comes again in glory,
we pray for the grace and honesty
to see what needs transforming
in our lives as individuals
and as members of the Church of God.

Silence

O come:
let us walk in the light of the Lord.

May all church leaders, pastors and teachers
be directed, inspired and upheld
by the living Spirit of God,
and may there be a deepening
of love and commitment
in all Christians the world over.

Silence

O come:
let us walk in the light of the Lord.

May the leaders of this nation
and of all the nations
be drawn increasingly to understand
God's ways of justice and righteousness,
and be filled with the longing
to do what is right and honest and good.

Silence

O come:
let us walk in the light of the Lord.

May all the families on earth
be blessed with mutual love
and caring consideration one of another;
may arguments and misunderstandings be properly resolved,
and difficult relationships refreshed and healed.

Silence

O come:
let us walk in the light of the Lord.

May those for whom the days and nights
creep past in pain or sorrow
be given comfort and hope;
may the frightened find reassurance
and the anxious find peace of mind.

Silence

O come:
let us walk in the light of the Lord.

May those who have reached the point of death
be given the knowledge of God's closeness
on that last journey;
and may those who have died
know the eternal peace and joy of heaven.

Silence

O come:
let us walk in the light of the Lord.

Mary's response prepared the way for our salvation;
we make our prayer with her:
Hail, Mary . . .

In the silence of God's stillness
we name any we know
who especially need our prayer.

Silence

Celebrant
Father, trusting in your mercy,
we lay these prayers before you,
through Jesus Christ our Lord.
Amen.

SECOND SUNDAY OF ADVENT

Get the road ready for the Lord!

Celebrant
Our God is always ready to hear our prayers.
Let us be still, and pray to him now.

Reader
In gratitude for all those who remind us
to be kind and loving by their words and example,
we pray for the Church throughout the world
and for our own community,
that we may be ready to welcome the Lord
and put right whatever blocks us from his love.

Silence

Come to us, Lord:
we know our need of you.

We pray that the lines of communication
between people and nations
may be kept open, respected and honoured,
and that where communication
has broken down
there may be a new desire for healing.

Silence

Come to us, Lord:
we know our need of you.

We pray for all those making and repairing roads,
travelling on them and stuck in traffic jams;
we pray for the towns and villages linked by roads,
for a public transport system
that protects the environment,
and serves the community.

Silence

Come to us, Lord:
we know our need of you.

We pray for those we see and talk to
every day or every week;
for those we often argue with
or misunderstand;
for those who brighten our lives
and make us smile;
for a greater thankfulness and appreciation
of those we usually take for granted.

Silence

Come to us, Lord:
we know our need of you.

We pray for those we have hurt or upset;
for those who feel isolated and alone;
for the ill, the frail, the stressed and the bitter.

Silence

Come to us, Lord:
we know our need of you.

We pray for the dying
and those who have died to this earthly life.
May they know the eternal peace of heaven,
and may those who miss them be comforted.

Silence

Come to us, Lord:
we know our need of you.

We make our prayer with Mary,
whose willing obedience
made our salvation possible:
Hail, Mary . . .

Together in silence
we make our private petitions
and thanksgivings.

Silence

Celebrant
Father of all time and place,
accept these prayers
through Christ, our Lord.
Amen.

THIRD SUNDAY OF ADVENT

Great expectations. Jesus fulfils the great statements of prophecy.

Celebrant
Knowing that our God loves us and listens,
let us pray to him now.

Reader
The Church is so full of possibility
and yet so vulnerable;
it is so urgently needed by our world
and yet often so weak;
We pray that the Lord may strengthen
each member of the body,
and increase our sense of expectation
so that we live with your life.

Silence

Faithful God:
you are the rock we stand on.

In our constantly changing world,
with its shifting values
and fragile ecological balance,
may we be rooted deeply in the Lord's unchanging nature
of mercy, goodness, faithfulness and love.

Silence

Faithful God:
you are the rock we stand on.

May we welcome the Lord into our homes,
our streets, and our communities;
where we are blind to his presence,
may he give us sight;
in the ordinary and the remarkable,
help us to recognise our true and living God.

Silence

Faithful God:
you are the rock we stand on.

With God-given love we bring to mind
those who are suffering physically,
spiritually or emotionally,
that they may find the Lord there beside them
in these dark and painful times.

Silence

Faithful God:
you are the rock we stand on.

We pray that the Lord, to whom eternity is natural,
may help us to realise
that time is not the whole story,
and welcome into his kingdom
those who have lived this life in his company
and have now passed through death;
may he comfort those of us here
whose hearts are heavy with grieving.

Silence

Faithful God:
you are the rock we stand on.

As we open our hearts to receive Jesus,
we remember Mary's receptive love,
and make our prayer with her:
Hail, Mary . . .

In the silence of our hearts
we pray to our heavenly Father
about our own particular concerns.

Silence

Celebrant
Lord, we ask you to hear these prayers
which we make through Jesus, our Saviour.
Amen.

Fourth Sunday of Advent

*Through the willing participation of Mary and Joseph,
God is poised to come among his people as their Saviour.*

Celebrant
Let us quieten ourselves to notice our God,
here with us now,
who is attentive to our deepest needs.

Reader
We long for our Church,
in its life and activity,
to be attentive to the Lord,
and ready to go wherever he suggests.
May he show us the work of the Church
from his point of view,
and develop our will to co-operate.

Silence

We call on your name, O God:
restore us and revive us.

We pray with longing for the kingdom
to come in our world,
and to flood with truth and love
the disillusion, hopelessness and terror
which traps the human spirit
and chokes its potential joy.

Silence

We call on your name, O God:
restore us and revive us.

We pray that the Lord will come into the daily relationships
we so easily take for granted,
and enable us to value one another,
delighting in one another's richness,
and responding to one another's needs with love.

Silence

We call on your name, O God:
restore us and revive us.

The Lord knows the need and pain
of those we love and worry about.
As he looks after them,
may he give them the sense of his caring presence
to uphold and sustain them.

Silence

We call on your name, O God:
restore us and revive us.

For us death can seem so cruel;
we ask for a better understanding of eternity.
May the Lord gather into his kingdom all those
whose earthly journey has come to an end.

Silence

We call on your name, O God:
restore us and revive us.

With Mary,
in whom the promise of the prophets
was fulfilled,
we make our prayer in hope and faith:
Hail, Mary . . .

Upheld by God's peace,
we pray now in silence
for any who specially need our prayers.

Silence

Celebrant
Father, we ask you to accept our prayers
through Jesus Christ, our Saviour.
Amen.

CHRISTMAS DAY

The Word of God is made flesh.
In the birth of Jesus we see God expressed in human terms.

Celebrant
As we celebrate the birth of Jesus,
the Word of God,
let us pray with thankful hearts.

Reader
The bells and lights and presents and decorations
in church and in our homes
express our thanks to the Lord,
for coming into the world in person.
May he bless us
and always keep us close to him.

Silence

On this Christmas Day we want to say:
Thank you, holy God!

The world Jesus was born into
was the world we know,
a world of dangers and risks.
In gratitude for his sharing our human weakness,
may his coming be a source of strength
to those in need.

Silence

On this Christmas Day we want to say:
Thank you, holy God!

Many of us will be celebrating
with our families and friends;
others will be at a distance from us.
May the Lord be with us all
and teach us true loving.

Silence

On this Christmas Day we want to say:
Thank you, holy God!

We pray for those who find Christmas
a sad or lonely season;
we pray for those for whom
it brings to the surface
memories, anxieties or dangers.
Through good and difficult times
we ask that the Lord be with us always.

Silence

On this Christmas Day we want to say:
Thank you, holy God!

We pray for those
whose loved ones have died,
and all those who have finished
with earthly celebrations.
May they celebrate with all the angels
in the joy of heaven.

Silence

On this Christmas Day we want to say:
Thank you, holy God!

Encouraged by Mary's example of love,
we join our prayers with hers:
Hail, Mary . . .

We pray in silence, now,
for our own particular needs and concerns.

Silence

Celebrant
Father, with thanks and joy
we offer these prayers
through Jesus our Saviour.
Amen.

FIRST SUNDAY OF CHRISTMAS: THE HOLY FAMILY

*Jesus, the expression of God's love, lives as a vulnerable
boy in the real and dangerous world we all inhabit.*

Celebrant
Let us pray to the God who travels with us
in all our celebrations and tragedies,
and understands what it is like to be human.

Reader
As we celebrate Christmas,
when the Word of God became flesh,
we pray for the Church, the Body of Christ.
May we be so filled with God's loving life
that our actions touch the world with hope
which lasts even when Christmas decorations
are put away.

Silence

Thank you, Lord God:
for coming to save us.

As the world is reminded of love and peace
in the words of the carols,
may the reality of a God who loves us so much
transform our social and political thinking,
and energise our plans and negotiations.

Silence

Thank you, Lord God:
for coming to save us.

As Christmas brings together
family members and friends,
and we make contact with those
we seldom meet,
may all our relationships be nourished
with love and forgiveness,
and may we value one another more.

Silence

Thank you, Lord God:
for coming to save us.

We remember all who are forced to escape
from their homes, and live without security;
we think particularly of those with young children
who are homeless or in danger.

Silence

Thank you, Lord God:
for coming to save us.

We pray for those whose earthly journey
has come to an end,
and those who have tended them during their dying;
we pray for those who have died through violence,
and for those who have much to forgive.

Silence

Thank you, Lord God:
for coming to save us.

With Mary,
who mothered the Son of God,
we make our prayer:
Hail, Mary . . .

In silence which God our Father
fills with accepting love,
we name those we know
who are in any particular need.

Silence

Celebrant
Heavenly Father,
we ask you to accept these prayers
which we make through Jesus, your Son.
Amen.

Second Sunday of Christmas

The grace and truth revealed in Jesus
show God's freely given love; through Jesus, God pours
out his blessings on us and gives us real freedom.

Celebrant
Let us settle ourselves in the stillness of God's peace
as we pray.

Reader
May the Church always be open
to the flood of the Father's love.
May he wash away all but what is
constructed out of his love
and built on his foundations.

Silence

O come:
let us adore.

May our world become sensitised
to hear the whispered voice
of God's love;
may we honour his creation
and value one another
as he values us.

Silence

O come:
let us adore.

May we receive the Lord
into our homes and families,
our shops, schools and places of work;
may we receive him into our conflicts,
our arguments and our expectations.

Silence

O come:
let us adore.

Even as we thank him for giving us free will,
we pray to the Father for those suffering
as a tragic result of wrong choices.
May they experience
his upholding and healing
in body and soul.

Silence

O come:
let us adore.

May those who are journeying
through death to eternity,
be awakened to the everlasting love
of God's Presence.

Silence

O come:
let us adore.

We join our prayers with those of Mary,
whose joy at the Incarnation we share:
Hail, Mary . . .

In the silence of God's attentive love,
we pray our private petitions.

Silence

Celebrant
Father, almighty and ever-present,
we commend our prayers to your mercy,
through Christ our Lord.
Amen.

THE EPIPHANY OF THE LORD

Jesus, the hope of the nations, is shown to the world.

Celebrant
We are all companions on a spiritual journey.
As we travel together, let us pray.

Reader
We pray that the worldwide Church
may always be ready
to travel in the way of the Lord
and in his direction.

Silence

Light of the world:
shine in our darkness.

We pray for the nations
as they live through conflicts
and struggle with identity.
We long for all peoples
to acknowledge the true and living God.

Silence

Light of the world:
shine in our darkness.

We pray for the families and the streets we represent,
asking for a spirit of generous love,
understanding and mutual respect.

Silence

Light of the world:
shine in our darkness.

We pray for all who are finding their way
tedious, lonely or frightening at the moment;
for those who have lost their way
and do not know what to do for the best.

Silence

Light of the world:
shine in our darkness.

We pray for those who have come
to the end of their earthly journey,
and for those who have died unprepared.

Silence

Light of the world:
shine in our darkness.

With Mary, Mother of Jesus,
let us pray:
Hail, Mary . . .

In silence,
as God our Father listens with love,
we name our own particular cares and concerns.

Silence

Celebrant
Heavenly Father,
we ask you to accept these prayers,
through Christ, our Saviour.
Amen.

THE BAPTISM OF THE LORD

*As Jesus is baptised, the Spirit of God
rest visibly on him, marking him out as the One
who will save his people.*

Celebrant
Let us attune our hearts to the God who loves us.

Reader
We pray to the God of love
for all those who are newly baptised,
or who have recently found that the Lord is real;
we pray for all in ordained and lay ministries,
and for those sensing a special calling.

Silence

In God:
all things work together for good.

We pray to the God of power
for those who are in authority
and in positions of influence and responsibility;
may they be earthed in humility,
courageous in integrity,
and mindful of the need to serve.

Silence

In God:
all things work together for good.

We call to mind those with whom we share
the work and leisure of our life;
we pray to the God of mercy
for those we treasure and those we battle with,
and ask him to breathe into all our relationships
the forgiving love which cleanses and heals.

Silence

In God:
all things work together for good.

We remember those who are aching today
in body, mind or spirit;
knowing that nothing is unredeemable,
we pray to the God of wholeness
that he will bring good even out of these barren places.

Silence

In God:
all things work together for good.

We pray to the God of life
for those whose earthly lives have ended;
we remember those who have died
violently and tragically, suddenly and unprepared.
We give thanks for lives well lived
and for happy memories.
May they rest in the eternal peace of heaven.

Silence

In God:
all things work together for good.

Now we join our prayers
with those of Mary, the Mother of Jesus:
Hail, Mary . . .

In the space of silence,
we bring to God our Father
our private petitions.

Silence

Celebrant
In thankfulness for all our blessings
we ask you, Father,
to hear our prayers, through Christ our Lord.
Amen.

FIRST SUNDAY OF LENT

Jesus knows all about temptation;
and he can deal with our sin.

Celebrant
Our God knows us and the temptations we face.
Let us pray to him now.

Reader
As the Church begins this season of Lent
may the Lord remind us of what is important
and what is not;
of where we are wandering away
and what we need to change;
so that by Easter
we will be renewed and strengthened
for service in the world.

Silence

The Lord is God:
there is no other.

The world's misery and pain
and desperate need of healing
are clear to see and affect us all.
We pray now for this damaged world
with all its weakness, longings and failings,
with all its potential and hope.

Silence

The Lord is God:
there is no other.

Whenever a child is born
we celebrate the creative hope of God.
We pray for all being born this week
and for their families and communities,
that all our children may be loved and cared for,
safe and happy.

Silence

The Lord is God:
there is no other.

We pray for all who suffer through others' sin;
all victims of abuse or oppression or apathy;
all whose adult lives are distorted and misshapen
by early damaging experiences
which need God's healing love.

Silence

The Lord is God:
there is no other.

We remember those who,
freed from the ageing and pain of their bodies,
can live now with the Lord
in the peace and joy of heaven.

Silence

The Lord is God:
there is no other.

We join our prayers with those of Mary,
whose Son has brought us salvation:
Hail, Mary . . .

In silence now,
we approach our loving Father
with our private petitions.

Silence

Celebrant
Father, accept these prayers,
through Jesus Christ our Lord.
Amen.

SECOND SUNDAY OF LENT

*The disciples witness the glory of God revealed in Jesus.
It is a glimpse of the glory which will be the great
hope for all nations of the world.*

Celebrant
As children together in the family of God,
let us pray now to our Father in heaven.

Reader
We pray that as Christians
we may listen more attentively
and with greater urgency than ever before
to the words of Jesus;
that we may be more aware of his presence with us,
both in our worship and in our daily ministry,
and that we may have the courage to live out his truth with joy.

Silence

Holy God:
transform us and use us to your glory.

We pray for those who do not know the Lord
or dismiss him as irrelevant to their lives;
we pray for those
who influence and encourage others
in what is evil, destructive or depraved,
and ask that the Lord give protection
to all who are vulnerable and in danger.

Silence

Holy God:
transform us and use us to your glory.

We pray for all who are adjusting
to new relationships in the family,
new homes or new work and leisure patterns;
we pray for stronger root growth in the Lord,
so that we are not thrown
by the changes and troubles of everyday life,
knowing the reality of his faithfulness.

Silence

Holy God:
transform us and use us to your glory.

We pray for all who are too exhausted
or overwhelmed by circumstances and pressures
to be able to pray;
may the Lord surround all those
who are troubled and heavily laden
with the revitalising assurance of your presence,
his understanding and his love.

Silence

Holy God:
transform us and use us to your glory.

We pray that those who have gone through death
may know the brightness of everlasting life;
may we, with them, come to experience
the glory and joy of heaven.

Silence

Holy God:
transform us and use us to your glory.

As we join our prayers with those of Mary,
may we learn from her responsive love:
Hail, Mary . . .

We pray in silence
for those known to us
who have particular needs.

Silence

Celebrant
Father, your glory fills the world,
and so we entrust our cares to you,
through Christ our Lord.
Amen.

THIRD SUNDAY OF LENT

God both knows us completely and loves us completely;
meeting us where we are, he provides us with living water,
to satisfy all our needs.

Celebrant
Thirsty for God, let us pray to him now,
in the knowledge that he will provide for us
in the way that is best.

Reader
Wherever the Church is dry and parched
may the water of the Spirit well up
to refresh and renew,
to bring life and strong new growth.
May the Lord make us more aware of our thirst for him,
so that we come to him ready and eager
to receive his living water.

Silence

Living God:
satisfy our thirst.

From the conflicting needs
and agendas of the world
we cry for mercy,
for a deeper understanding of one another
and a greater desire for co-operation and peace.
We pray for sensitivity
in handling delicate negotiations
and the wisdom which respects and listens.

Silence

Living God:
satisfy our thirst.

We pray that in all our relationships
we may be made effective channels
of the Lord's love and forgiveness.
May he make us awash with living water

so that our homes and places of work,
our shopping and leisure centres,
our conversations and actions,
are always in touch with his renewing power.

Silence

Living God:
satisfy our thirst.

We stand alongside all those who are suffering,
whether in body, mind or spirit,
and long for healing and comfort,
for strength for perseverance
and for patience in the dark times;
we long for the living Spirit to envelop and sustain them.

Silence

Living God:
satisfy our thirst.

We pray for those who have come
to the end of earthly life.
May they, placing their faith in the God of life,
share in the light and joy of heaven for ever.

Silence

Living God:
satisfy our thirst.

We make our prayer with Mary,
faithful Mother of Jesus:
Hail, Mary . . .

Now, in silence,
we pray our individual petitions
to our heavenly Father,
who has promised to hear us.

Silence

Celebrant
Christ is among us,
and through him we offer these prayers
to you, our heavenly Father.
Amen.

FOURTH SUNDAY OF LENT

*Jesus gives sight to the man born blind and exposes
the blindness of those who claim to see.*

Celebrant
Let us open our hearts to God
and pray to him for the Church and for the world.

Reader
In our blindness we come to the Lord
for insight and perception,
for discernment and vision;
may we focus our gaze on his glory
in constant wonder and praise
until we see with his eyes
and notice with his love.

Silence

Open our eyes:
so that we can see.

Wherever our world is damaged
or communities torn apart
by prejudice, narrow-mindedness,
or the refusal to see injustice or recognise needs,
may the Lord anoint eyes and hearts to see with honesty
and act with integrity and compassion.

Silence

Open our eyes:
so that we can see.

May the Lord help us to see things from different perspectives,
and from one another's viewpoint,
so that we learn input as well as output,
listening as well as speaking,
the joy of giving as well as the humility of receiving;
may we reverence one another
in all our conversations,
both face to face and when discussing those who are absent.

Silence

Open our eyes:
so that we can see.

We pray for all who are blind and poorly sighted,
that they may be kept safe from danger
and enabled to live full lives;
we ask that the Lord bless those working to remove cataracts
for the poor in the Third World and restore their sight.
We pray for those who are spiritually blind;
for those blinded by rage and hurt,
jealousy or complacency.

Silence

Open our eyes:
so that we can see.

We commend to the Lord's safe-keeping for ever
all who have died in faith,
and all who have been working in his service
though they did not know him by name;
as they see him face to face
may their joy fill eternity.

Silence

Open our eyes:
so that we can see.

In our praise we join with Mary and say:
Hail, Mary . . .

We name in silence now
any known to us
with particular needs or burdens.

Silence

Celebrant
Loving Father, we bring you these prayers
through Christ our Lord,
and through him we offer ourselves
to be used in your service.
Amen.

FIFTH SUNDAY OF LENT

Jesus is the resurrection and the life.
He can transform death and despair,
in any form, into life and hope.

Celebrant
As the people of the living God,
let us join together in our prayers
for the Church and for the world.

Reader
May God breathe his life into the Church;
breathe holiness and deepening faith,
breathe energy, inspired teaching and fervent praise;
may he unblock the channels and make us more receptive
to his gentleness and his power.

Silence

Breathe into us:
so that we live in you.

May God breathe his life into the universe;
breathe caring, honesty and compassion,
breathe right values and good stewardship,
peace and reconciliation, vision and hope.

Silence

Breathe into us:
so that we live in you.

May God breathe his life
into our homes and places of work;
breathe increased patience and understanding,
and the courage to live the Christian life,
when to do so brings ridicule or demands sacrifice.

Silence

Breathe into us:
so that we live in you.

May God breathe his life into those who suffer;
breathe comfort and wholeness,
forgiveness and new confidence,
breathe peace of mind
and the knowledge of his love.

Silence

Breathe into us:
so that we live in you.

May God breathe his life into the dead and dying;
breathe courage for the journey
and the realisation that he can be trusted.
May he breathe life that lasts for ever.

Silence

Breathe into us:
so that we live in you.

We join our prayers with those of Mary,
the Mother of our Saviour:
Hail, Mary . . .

Trustingly we pray in silence
to our loving Lord,
who considers each one of us special.

Silence

Celebrant
Father, we thank you for your constant love,
and offer these prayers
through your Son, Jesus Christ, our Lord.
Amen.

Palm (Passion) Sunday

Jesus rides into Jerusalem cheered by the crowds.
Days later, crowds will be clamouring for his death.

Celebrant
As we recall the extent of God's love for us,
let us pray.

Reader
If we as the Church
are truly to be the Body of Christ,
then, standing at the foot of the cross,
may we learn what it means to love
and keep on loving;
to serve and keep on serving.

Silence

God our Father:
let your will be done in us.

If the world is ever to see real hope,
may the Lord purify and transform our lives
and stretch out our arms in loving forgiveness,
with no exceptions and no small print,
so that we shine as lights in the darkness.

Silence

God our Father:
let your will be done in us.

If our workplaces and neighbourhoods and homes
are to display and respond to his values,
then may the Lord make us more fervent in prayer,
more courageous in self-discipline
and, above all, more loving in reaching out to them.

Silence

God our Father:
let your will be done in us.

If the terrible suffering of extreme poverty,
injustice and oppression
is to be addressed realistically,
then may the Lord take away our greed and complacency
and our assumptions about appropriate living standards,
and teach us sacrificial self-giving
of time, energy and resources.

Silence

God our Father:
let your will be done in us.

Through the life-giving death of Jesus,
may the dying turn to the Father
and know his merciful love;
may the grieving be comforted,
and may we all one day share
with those who have died
the eternal joy of heaven.

Silence

God our Father:
let your will be done in us.

With Mary, the bearer of God's Son,
we make our prayer:
Hail, Mary . . .

Knowing that God our Father
hears the cry of his children,
we pray in silence for our own needs and cares.

Silence

Celebrant
Merciful Father,
we know that you hold all life in your hand;
please hear our prayers,
through Jesus our Redeemer.
Amen.

EASTER DAY

It is true. Jesus is alive for all time.
The Lord of life cannot be held by death. God's victory over
sin and death means that new life for us is a reality.

Celebrant
As we celebrate the new life of Resurrection,
let us pray to the one true God,
who brings us all to life.

Reader
We pray that the Church may proclaim with joy
the Easter message of hope for the world;
may our lives, as well as our worship,
testify to the truth of the Resurrection;
and may our vision of what is possible
through this new life be broadened.

Silence

Life-giving God:
transform our lives.

We pray for the world we inhabit;
for those who lead, and take important decisions,
and for those who follow or are coerced,
or who have no voice.
We pray for mercy and justice,
compassion and integrity.
We pray for protection against evil
and strengthening of goodness.

Silence

Life-giving God:
transform our lives.

We pray for all babies,
and those as yet unborn,
that they may be born into a world
of love and acceptance.

We pray, too, for those who provide foster care,
and for all children at risk.
We pray for all parents and those who support them.
We pray for the newly baptised
and recently confirmed;
for a deeper commitment to supporting one another
as we grow in faith.

Silence

Life-giving God:
transform our lives.

We pray for those who cannot think,
for the pain or anguish which engulfs them;
for all whose lives are troubled and insecure;
for those who have little energy left to rejoice.
May the risen Lord bring healing
and the resources to cope with suffering,
and give us the grace
to carry one another's burdens in love.

Silence

Life-giving God:
transform our lives.

We make our prayer with Mary,
who knew the cost of loving:
Hail, Mary . . .

In the silence of God's accepting love,
we pray our individual petitions.

Silence

Celebrant
In silence we praise you, Father,
for your abundant blessings,
and ask you to hear these prayers
which we make through Jesus Christ, our risen Lord.
Amen.

SECOND SUNDAY OF EASTER

Through the risen Jesus we have a living hope
which will never spoil or fade.

Celebrant
As we gather here
with God's presence in the midst of us,
let us pray.

Reader
We bring to the Lord
the Church in all its richness and all its need;
all its diversity and all its division.
May he give us a fresh understanding
of what it means to live in him;
may all of us celebrate the reality
of his presence among us,
filling us with new life and new hope.

Silence

Lord in your presence:
we lift our hearts to you.

We bring to the Lord
all those areas of our lives and our world
where there is confusion and bewilderment;
may he help us to go beyond our doubts and insecurity,
and to experience the joy of his peace.

Silence

Lord in your presence:
we lift our hearts to you.

We bring to the Lord
our homes and families,
and all the joys and sorrows
of our relationships.
We ask him to be with us
in all we say and do.

Silence

Lord in your presence:
we lift our hearts to you.

We bring to the Lord
those whom life has damaged,
and all who find it difficult to trust in him;
may he give them refreshment and hope,
comfort, healing and inner serenity.

Silence

Lord in your presence:
we lift our hearts to you.

We bring to the Lord
those who approach death with great fear
and those who die unprepared to meet him.
May he have mercy on us all,
forgive us all that is past
and gather us into his everlasting kingdom
of peace and joy.

Silence

Lord in your presence:
we lift our hearts to you.

Remembering Mary's dedication and love,
we make our prayer with her:
Hail, Mary . . .

Knowing that God loves us personally
and with full understanding,
we make our private petitions
to him in silence.

Silence

Celebrant
Father, coming together with thanks and praise
to worship you,
we ask you to accept these prayers
which we make through Christ our Lord.
Amen.

Third Sunday of Easter

*Jesus explains the scriptures and is
recognised in the breaking of bread.*

Celebrant
As we gather to hear the word of God
and to break bread in the presence of Jesus,
let us pray.

Reader
May the Lord walk with us on our journey of faith,
both as individuals and as the Church of God;
open up to us the truths
he longs for us to understand,
and inspire all who teach and encourage
to pass on the good news of Easter.

Silence

Lord God:
abide with us.

May the Lord walk with us down the streets
of our cities, towns and villages,
drive with us down the motorways
and fly with us down the air corridors.
May he meet all those who are curious, searching,
or moving in the wrong direction.
May his presence be sought
and recognised in all the world.

Silence

Lord God:
abide with us.

May the Lord walk with us in our life journeys,
guiding, teaching and correcting us,
as we learn the lessons of loving
in our homes, our work and our communities.

Silence

Lord God:
abide with us.

May the Lord walk with us
through the times of suffering and pain,
alerting us to one another's needs
and providing for us
in whatever ways are best for us.
May he help us to trust him through the dark times,
and breathe new life and hope
into those who are close to despair.

Silence

Lord God:
abide with us.

May the Lord walk with us through the valley of death;
may our love and prayers support those
who walk that journey today.
May he draw close to them and welcome them
into the joy of heaven.

Silence

Lord God:
abide with us.

May we learn from the humility of Mary
as we pray with her to the God of heaven:
Hail, Mary . . .

Confident in God's welcoming love,
we pray in silence, now,
for our individual needs.

Silence

Celebrant
Father, in silence, we adore you,
and open ourselves to your healing love.
Accept us, and our prayers, dear Father,
for the sake of Jesus, the Christ.
Amen.

FOURTH SUNDAY OF EASTER

*Jesus, the Good Shepherd, has come so that
we may have life in rich abundance.*

Celebrant
The Lord is our shepherd,
and we are the sheep of his pasture.
Let us bring to him our cares and concerns
for the Church and for the world.

Reader
We pray to the Good Shepherd of the sheep
for the Church;
for all congregations, for pastors
and all who minister in word and sacrament;
we pray particularly for bishops
in their shepherding of the world Church.
We pray for clear guidance and direction
in those issues which disturb us,
asking not to be led in the easy way
but in the way that is right and good.

Silence

The Lord is my shepherd:
there is nothing I shall want.

We pray to the Good Shepherd of the sheep
for the world we inhabit –
the world we have inherited
and will pass on to successive generations.
May he teach us to look after it carefully and wisely,
to share its gifts more fairly,
and work together to ease its sufferings.
May he turn the hearts of those who are excited by evil things
and encourage the timid to speak out
for what is wholesome and good.

Silence

The Lord is my shepherd:
there is nothing I shall want.

We pray to the Good Shepherd of the sheep for our places of work,
our colleagues, friends and neighbours,
and the members of our families.
We ask not for popularity at all costs,
but the grace to do his will and to be his witnesses
to what it means to live lovingly,
both when this is easy and also when it hurts.

Silence

The Lord is my shepherd:
there is nothing I shall want.

We pray to the Good Shepherd of the sheep for the weak and vulnerable,
for those who must live depending on others for every need,
and for those who are bullied, or constantly despised.
We pray for a greater reverence, one for another,
for a greater willingness to uphold and encourage one another;
we pray for healing and wholeness.

Silence

The Lord is my shepherd:
there is nothing I shall want.

We pray to the Good Shepherd of the sheep for those who have died;
we pray for those who ache with sorrow at their going;
we commend them all into his unfailing care
which lasts throughout this life and on into eternity.

Silence

The Lord is my shepherd:
there is nothing I shall want.

We make our prayer with Mary,
who was so open to God's will:
Hail, Mary . . .

In a time of silence we share with God our Father
our personal burdens, joys and sorrows.

Silence

Celebrant
Father, we bring you our cares and concerns,
and ask you to hear these prayers
through Jesus Christ.
Amen.

FIFTH SUNDAY OF EASTER

Jesus is the Way, the Truth and the Life,
through whom we can come into the presence of God for ever.

Celebrant
As living stones,
let us pray for the building up of God's Church,
and for the world God loves.

Reader
Through the power of his Spirit,
may the Living God build us up
into a spiritual temple where he is glorified day after day,
in all our praise and worship,
and in our love for one another.

Silence

You are my strong rock:
my strong rock and my shelter.

May our consciences be sharpened
to sense the direction of the Living God;
may he protect us from all that draws us away from him.
May he guide our leaders in the way of truth
and in the values which are built on him.

Silence

You are my strong rock:
my strong rock and my shelter.

May the Way which Jesus shows us
be the Way we live out our daily lives
around the table, in the daylight and the dark,
in the misunderstandings, the tensions and the rush,
in the eye contact,
the conversations and the growing.

Silence

You are my strong rock:
my strong rock and my shelter.

We lay before the Living God
those who are travelling through a time
of pain or anguish, tragedy or conflict
which is hard to bear.
We stand alongside them in their suffering,
and ask that the Lord give them
his transforming, healing love.

Silence

You are my strong rock:
my strong rock and my shelter.

We remember those who have died
and pray for them now.
May the Lord lead them out of their pain
into the light of eternity,
and keep us all in the Way that leads us
to share that everlasting life.

Silence

You are my strong rock:
my strong rock and my shelter.

Mindful of Mary's quiet
and prayerful acceptance of God's will,
we join our prayers with hers:
Hail, Mary . . .

As our loving Father listens in love,
we pray our own petitions
in silence and stillness.

Silence

Celebrant
Merciful Father,
we ask you to accept our prayers
which we make through Christ, our Lord.
Amen.

SIXTH SUNDAY OF EASTER

The Spirit of truth, given to us,
enables us to discern the living, risen Christ.

Celebrant
As we gather in the company of the living God,
let us pray.

Reader
We pray that the Church
may be alive with the risen life of the Lord,
refreshed and revived by the breath of the Spirit,
purified and refined like gold and silver,
so that we truly offer the possibility
of saving love to the searching world.

Silence

You are the one true God:
and we worship you.

We pray that in all meetings and conferences
where important decisions are taken,
hearts may be turned to honour what is just and true,
compassionate and constructive.
We pray that in all areas
where there is corruption, deceit or distrust,
consciences may be sensitised afresh
to know what is right and strive towards it.

Silence

You are the one true God:
and we worship you.

We pray for the streets
and places of work we represent.
May they be places where the truth of the Lord's being
is proclaimed daily by the way we live
and handle the everyday situations, through his leading.
May our words and actions speak of his faithful love,
graciousness and purity.

Silence

You are the one true God:
and we worship you.

We pray for all who feel out of their depth,
all who are drowning in their pain, sorrow or guilt.
May the Lord of life set them free and save them,
support them to a place of safety
and fix their feet on the solid rock of his love.

Silence

You are the one true God:
and we worship you.

We pray for those who have died;
may they now see the Lord of life as he really is.
We ask for mercy and forgiveness,
and commend them to his keeping for ever.

Silence

You are the one true God:
and we worship you.

We pray with Mary
who, in wonder and trust,
accepted the impossible:
Hail, Mary . . .

In silence we bring the individual names
of any who have hurt us, or those we love,
to the healing power of God.

Silence

Celebrant
Father of mercy,
look compassionately on your children
and hear us as we pray, through Christ.
Amen.

THE ASCENSION OF THE LORD

Having bought back our freedom with the giving of his life,
Jesus enters into the full glory to which he is entitled.

Celebrant
As we celebrate together,
let us pray together.

Reader
As we celebrate this festival
of Jesus' entry into heaven as Saviour and Lord,
we pray for unity in the Church
and reconciliation and renewed vision.

Silence

Both heaven and earth:
are full of God's glory.

As we recall the shout of praise in heaven
as the Lamb of God appears,
we pray for all who are hailed as heroes
and given great honour on earth;
for all who worship anyone or anything
other than the true God.

Silence

Both heaven and earth:
are full of God's glory.

We pray for all farewells and homecomings
among our families and in our community,
and for all who have lost touch with loved ones
and long for reunion.

Silence

Both heaven and earth:
are full of God's glory.

We pray for those who are full of tears,
and cannot imagine being happy again;
we pray for the hardened and callous,
whose inner hurts have never yet been healed.
We pray for wholeness and comfort and new life.

Silence

Both heaven and earth:
are full of God's glory.

We commend to the Father's eternal love
those we remember who have died,
and we pray too for those
who miss their physical presence.

Silence

Both heaven and earth:
are full of God's glory.

We make our prayer with Mary,
who, in joy, poured out her thanks and praise:
Hail, Mary . . .

God our Father loves us;
in silence we pray
our personal petitions to him now.

Silence

Celebrant
Father, trusting in your great love for us,
we bring you these prayers
through Jesus Christ our Lord.
Amen.

Seventh Sunday of Easter

God's glory is often revealed in the context
of suffering and failure in the world's eyes.

Celebrant
As the Church of God,
let us be still, and pray together.

Reader
We pray that the God of glory
may make his light shine in our church community
as he works among us
and blesses us with his presence;
with gratitude for the gifts he has given us,
we ask him to bless our various ministries.

Silence

Holy God:
may we live with your life in us.

May the whole world come to know the God of glory
and give him honour and praise.
May he encourage us all to stand up to the devil,
firm in our faith,
and strengthened with his power.

Silence

Holy God:
may we live with your life in us.

May our homes, schools, shops, offices and factories
become places where the God of glory
is seen and experienced
in the ordinary things and the everyday routines.
May he fill us to overflowing with ongoing thankfulness
both in the sunlight and in the storm.

Silence

Holy God:
may we live with your life in us.

Confident in his special affection
for the discarded and marginalised,
the weak and the vulnerable,
we pray to the God of glory for all those
who find life an exhausting struggle,
or who long for some respite from pain or depression.
May he support them in their troubles,
bring healing and reassurance,
and touch them with the gentleness of his peace.

Silence

Holy God:
may we live with your life in us.

May the God of glory teach us to understand death
in the context of his eternity,
so that our fears are calmed as we approach it.
May he welcome with merciful love those who have recently died
and shelter their loved ones, too,
in the shadow of his wings.

Silence

Holy God:
may we live with your life in us.

Mary's example teaches us
the power of loving response;
with her we make our prayer:
Hail, Mary . . .

In silence, now,
we pour out to God our Father
any needs and burdens known to us personally.

Silence

Celebrant
Father Almighty, take us by the hand
and lead us in your ways of peace and love;
we ask you to hear our prayers,
which we make through Christ, our Lord.
Amen.

Pentecost

*With great power the Spirit of God is
poured out on the expectant disciples.*

Celebrant
As the Body of Christ,
in the power of the Spirit,
let us pray.

Reader
For a fresh outpouring of the Holy Spirit
on the people of God
all over the world,
and in all worship traditions.
For a readiness to be changed and made new;
for a softening of the ground of our hearts
to receive without fear.

Silence

With our whole selves we pray:
come, Holy Spirit of God.

For all the peoples of the earth
to know and honour God's holy name.
For the healing of the nations
and a new thirst for righteousness and purity
at every level and in every aspect of society.
For a dissatisfaction with the pursuit of pleasure
and all that distracts us from our true calling.

Silence

With our whole selves we pray:
come, Holy Spirit of God.

For the grace and power to live out our faith
in the real and challenging world,
among those we meet and eat with,
whose lives we share,
without compromising that calling
to be the Body of Christ,

living God's integrity and purity,
forgiveness and love.

Silence

With our whole selves we pray:
come, Holy Spirit of God.

For those whose lives feel empty or cheated,
or filled with pain, or worry or guilt.
For all whose hopes and dreams are in tatters;
all who are in any way imprisoned.

Silence

With our whole selves we pray:
come, Holy Spirit of God.

For those who walk the dark journey of death
and all who have come through it
into God's presence;
for mourners distressed by regrets
or angry with God at their loss.

Silence

With our whole selves we pray:
come, Holy Spirit of God.

We pray with Mary,
Mother of the Church:
Hail, Mary . . .

Together in silence,
we name those known to us
who need our prayers.

Silence

Celebrant
Father, in grateful thanks
for all your blessings in our lives,
we relinquish our wills to yours,
and ask you to accept these prayers
through Christ our Lord.
Amen.

TRINITY SUNDAY

The mystery of God – Creator, Redeemer and Sanctifier
all at once – is beyond our human understanding,
yet closer to us than breathing.

Celebrant
Called by the great God we worship,
let us pray fervently for the Church
and for the world.

Reader
We bring before the Lord
the needs of the Church,
in its weakness and its potential;
that he may revive and refresh us, teach and direct us,
inspire all who preach, teach
and gossip the good news,
and uphold all who suffer for their faith in any way.

Silence

God of mystery and compassion:
you know us and you love us.

We bring before the Lord
the particular problems of our age and our culture;
that he may renew in us a commitment
to community and mutual trust,
and give a sense of value to all
who despise others and themselves.
May he protect the vulnerable and sensitise the hearts
of all who have become anaesthetised
by images of violence.

Silence

God of mystery and compassion:
you know us and you love us.

We bring before the Lord
the nurturing of our children and young people,
in homes and parenting, schools and teaching,

in the expectations, pressures and dangers,
in the hopes and possibilities for good.

Silence

God of mystery and compassion:
you know us and you love us.

We bring before the Lord
the hungry and malnourished,
the greedy and complacent;
those who are ill and those who care for them;
the unhappy and those who comfort them;
all who are undergoing surgery or painful treatment,
and all who have no one to turn to.

Silence

God of mystery and compassion:
you know us and you love us.

We bring before the Lord
those who have died in faith
and will now see him face to face;
those for whom death speaks of fear or annihilation,
and those who are unprepared.

Silence

God of mystery and compassion:
you know us and you love us.

With Mary, who, in loving obedience,
made herself available to God's will,
let us make our prayer:
Hail, Mary . . .

Together in silence,
we name those known to us
who need our prayers.

Silence

Celebrant
Father Almighty,
in the Spirit we pray,
and ask you to hear our prayers
through Jesus Christ our Lord.
Amen.

Corpus Christi

Jesus Christ is the living bread;
as we feed on him we share his life.

Celebrant
Gathered as the Body of Christ,
let us pray together to our heavenly Father.

Reader
We pray for all who celebrate
the Eucharistic mysteries,
all who administer the sacrament
of the body and blood of Christ,
and all who receive it, day by day,
week by week and year by year.
Through the loving nature of this feeding
may we all grow in holiness
and bring Christ's life to all we meet.

Silence

In our need:
we come to you.

We pray that all who know
their hunger and thirst for real feeding
may find the spiritual nourishment they crave,
and receive new and satisfying life
through Christ our Lord.
We pray that the world may know God's love for it.

Silence

In our need:
we come to you.

We pray for the spiritual feeding of our families,
and our parish family, through word and sacrament;
may we daily draw closer to the God who loves us,
and our lives become increasingly filled with his life
as we feed on him.

Silence

In our need:
we come to you.

We pray for those who, through frailty or illness,
receive the sacrament in their homes or in hospital;
for all who are malnourished or starving,
whether physically, emotionally or spiritually.

Silence

In our need:
we come to you.

We pray for those who have died,
that in mercy they may be brought
into the eternal joy of heaven.

Silence

In our need:
we come to you.

We make our prayers with Mary,
who brought the living bread into the world:
Hail, Mary . . .

Let us be still in the presence of God
and bring to him the needs and concerns
that weigh on our hearts.

Silence

Celebrant
Heavenly Father, hear our prayers and provide for us all;
as you nourish us by the body and blood of Jesus,
may we share the life of heaven,
both now and at the end of time.
Amen.

SECOND SUNDAY OF THE YEAR

*Jesus is recognised and pointed out
by John to be God's chosen one.*

Celebrant
Let us voice our cares and concerns,
knowing that God is listening to us.

Reader
We pray that the Lord may make himself known
to the people who come into our churches,
or who pass by and sometimes wonder,
but have not yet come in;
may we be better bearers of his life
to those who need him
but have never met him.

Silence

True and living God:
we want to know you more.

As the world lurches from crisis to crisis,
and there is much misleading and misdirecting,
we pray that the Lord may help us recover
the natural sense of what is right and just, honest and good,
so that our hearts are inclined
to hear the voice of his leading and respond to it.

Silence

True and living God:
we want to know you more.

We pray that the Lord will help us
to take more seriously our responsibility
of helping one another forward into faith,
as brothers and sisters;
we pray for those in our own families
whom we would love to bring to know the Lord,
and for those who have drifted away.

Silence

True and living God:
we want to know you more.

There are some who are going through
very distressing, painful and worrying times.
We stand alongside them now,
and ask the Lord to give them his comfort, reassurance,
healing and peace of mind.

Silence

True and living God:
we want to know you more.

Even as we pray now,
there are those journeying through death.
We pray for them, for all who have recently died,
and for all those left without their loved ones,
grieving, or numbed with shock.

Silence

True and living God:
we want to know you more.

Mary opened her life
to the loving power of God;
we now join our prayers with hers:
Hail, Mary . . .

In the silence of God's stillness,
we name any we know
who especially need our prayer.

Silence

Celebrant
God our Father,
you know us better than we know ourselves;
we ask you to hear our prayers
through Jesus Christ, your Son.
Amen.

THIRD SUNDAY OF THE YEAR

*The prophecies of Isaiah are fulfilled in a
new and lasting way in Jesus of Nazareth.*

Celebrant
Let us pray to the loving God we have seen in Jesus.

Reader
We pray that the light of God
will shine in the Church throughout the world,
to set us free from prejudice,
small-mindedness and hypocrisy.
As members of the Body of Christ
may we move freely through the power of God
wherever we are called to go,
available and active in God's service.

Silence

Lord God of power:
set us free to live.

We pray that our world may be lit
by this light in the darkness
to bring freedom and hope
wherever there is oppression,
recognition and respect where there is none,
and in all conflicts
positive ways forward.

Silence

Lord God of power:
set us free to live.

We pray that in our homes, our workplaces
and our neighbourhoods
the light of godly loving may soften harsh edges,
encourage mutual caring,
and heal dysfunctional or damaging relationships.

Silence

Lord God of power:
set us free to live.

We pray that all those
whose lives are fettered by the past,
by rejection, guilt, pain or anxiety,
may be set free and encouraged to live to the full.

Silence

Lord God of power:
set us free to live.

We pray for those who have died,
and those who miss them
and are finding it very hard to cope with their loss.
We pray for all those who have no one to help them
through that last journey.

Silence

Lord God of power:
set us free to live.

We join our prayers with those of Mary,
who ministered to her Son:
Hail, Mary . . .

We pray for our own needs and concerns
in silence to God our Father.

Silence

Celebrant
Father,
rejoicing in the richness of your love,
we ask you to accept these prayers,
through Christ our Lord.
Amen.

Fourth Sunday of the Year

Happy are the poor in spirit,
who are aware of their need of God.

Celebrant
Let us settle ourselves to stillness as we pray.

Reader
We ask not for ease and comfort
but the disturbing power of God's truth
and the challenge of his committed love,
so that as a Church we may be prepared
to move at his bidding and act on his will.

Silence

In our need:
we cry to you, O God.

We ask not for the riches to fall in our favour
but for right sharing
and just distribution of resources.
We ask not to be cocooned against reality
but strengthened to work for peace and justice
and trained to discern what is right and good.

Silence

In our need:
we cry to you, O God.

We ask not so much to receive
as for the grace to give with generosity
and to recover the joy of living simply,
contentedly and open to the guiding of the Lord.

Silence

In our need:
we cry to you, O God.

We stand alongside all
with great needs, hurts and troubles;
we ask the Lord to lay his hands
on those we mention now by name
in the silence of our hearts.

Silence

In our need:
we cry to you, O God.

We commend to the mercy
and loving kindness of the Father
those who have reached the end of their earthly life
and step into the realm of eternity.
May they be surrounded with his joy for ever.

Silence

In our need:
we cry to you, O God.

We pray with Mary,
so full of God's grace:
Hail, Mary . . .

As God's stillness fills our hearts,
we pray for our own cares and concerns.

Silence

Celebrant
Father, we lay before you these prayers,
and ask you to accept them
through Jesus, your Son.
Amen.

FIFTH SUNDAY OF THE YEAR

*We are commissioned to live so that we shine like lights
which direct others on to God, the source of Light.*

Celebrant
Let us pray to the God who has drawn us here today,
who loves us, and loves our world.

Reader
We pray that there may be a revival of longing
for the kingdom to come,
and a renewed commitment to working for it;
for a desire to live out our faith and worship
in our daily lives this week.

Silence

Come, Holy Spirit:
set our hearts on fire.

We pray that all who have authority and power
in our nation and our world
may use it for good,
upholding and instigating what is right and fair,
and listening to the needs of those they represent.
May we recognise our responsibility
to support and stand up for God's values.

Silence

Come, Holy Spirit:
set our hearts on fire.

We pray that within our homes and communities
there may be a new awareness
of one another's gifts and needs,
more sensitivity and respect in our relationships;
may we reverence one another as fellow beings,
born of the Father's creative love.

Silence

Come, Holy Spirit:
set our hearts on fire.

We pray for all who are oppressed,
downtrodden or despised;
we pray for those who will not eat today
and all who live in the degrading circumstances
of poverty and powerlessness;
we pray for a heart to put injustices right
and strive for a fair sharing of resources.

Silence

Come, Holy Spirit:
set our hearts on fire.

We pray for those whose life expectancy is short,
for the babies and children who have died
while we have been praying;
for all who have come to the end of their earthly life
and made that last journey through death;
may the father welcome them in his mercy
with the fullness of eternal life.

Silence

Come, Holy Spirit:
set our hearts on fire.

Joining with Mary,
who brought the Light into the world,
we make our prayer:
Hail, Mary . . .

In silence now,
we make our personal petitions to God,
who is always ready to hear us.

Silence

Celebrant
Father, God of love,
increase our love for one another,
and hear us as we pray.
We ask this through Christ our Lord.
Amen.

SIXTH SUNDAY OF THE YEAR

To live God's way is to choose the way of life.

Celebrant
Gathered together in one spirit,
let us pray to our God.

Reader
Wherever our attention has wandered from his calling,
wherever we have fallen short of his will for us,
and failed to keep the spirit of his law of love,
we pray that the Father may forgive us and transform us,
so that we walk again
the path that leads to life.

Silence

Show us the way of life:
and help us to walk in it.

Wherever the Church is asked
to give leadership on sensitive issues;
whenever the current world expectations of behaviour
need to be challenged in the light of God's love,
we pray for the wisdom and guidance we need.

Silence

Show us the way of life:
and help us to walk in it.

Wherever our homes are lacking
in love and mutual respect,
wherever destructive relationships
cause distress and heartache,
and wherever people are made to feel they don't matter,
may the Lord give a new realisation of his ways
and his hopes for us
so that his kingdom may come
and his will be done.

Silence

Show us the way of life:
and help us to walk in it.

Wherever there is illness, unhappiness,
injustice or fear;
wherever people feel frustrated,
imprisoned or trapped;
may the Lord give us a greater sense of loving community,
a heart to put right whatever we can,
and the willingness to stand
alongside one another in our sorrows.

Silence

Show us the way of life:
and help us to walk in it.

Wherever earthly lives have come to an end,
and people are grieving the loss of their loved ones,
may the Father fill these places
with the eternal peace of his presence,
and prepare us all through our lives on this earth
for everlasting life with him in heaven.

Silence

Show us the way of life:
and help us to walk in it.

We make our prayer with Mary,
who loved God with all her mind and heart:
Hail, Mary . . .

In this silence,
we approach our loving Father
with our private petitions.

Silence

Celebrant
Father, we ask you to hear our prayers,
for the love of Jesus, your Son.
Amen.

SEVENTH SUNDAY OF THE YEAR

We are called to be holy;
to be perfect in our generous loving,
because that is what God our Father is like.

Celebrant
God has chosen to call us here
and we have chosen to come.
Let us pray to him now.

Reader
We pray for stronger faith
and the courage to live up to our calling;
for the grace to act always
with a generosity of spirit,
until the whole Church models the wisdom
which the world counts as foolishness.

Silence

Holy God:
we commit ourselves to your service.

We pray for all the unresolved conflicts in our world.
We ask the Lord to give us his desire for peace,
his spirit of discernment,
his understanding of unspoken needs,
and his capacity for forgiveness.

Silence

Holy God:
we commit ourselves to your service.

We pray for the homes and families we represent,
and for all with whom we live and work.
May we recognise the opportunities
for generous, loving service
and put aside any destructive possessiveness
or self-interest.

Silence

Holy God:
we commit ourselves to your service.

We pray for peace of mind and spirit
in all those who are distressed or enveloped in pain.
May they know the reality of inner healing,
and may even the worst situations
become places of growth and new life.

Silence

Holy God:
we commit ourselves to your service.

We pray for those approaching death
with fear, resentment and anger,
and for all who counsel the dying and the bereaved.
We pray that those who have died will know
the joy of everlasting life.

Silence

Holy God:
we commit ourselves to your service.

With Mary, who was full of grace,
we make our prayer:
Hail, Mary . . .

As God's stillness fills our hearts,
we pray for any needs known to us personally.

Silence

Celebrant
We rededicate ourselves
to your love, Father,
and ask you to hear our prayers,
through Jesus Christ.
Amen.

EIGHTH SUNDAY OF THE YEAR

God is creative and good;
seeking his rule, as our priority,
will mean that everything else falls into place.

Celebrant
Let us pray to the God who knows us so well
and understands our needs.

Reader
In all the daily concerns of parish life,
and in the great issues facing the whole Church,
may we never lose sight of God's priorities
but see everything through the eyes of compassion,
with honesty and integrity.

Silence

Lord of creation:
let your kingdom come!

In the local issues of this community,
and in the difficulties and dilemmas
on the world stage,
may we look for the face of Christ
and fix our attention on his underlying values
of love, justice and mercy.

Silence

Lord of creation:
let your kingdom come!

In all the minor squabbles
and major rifts of family life,
may we know the assurance of Christ's promise
to be with us always,
and his power to transform and renew.

Silence

Lord of creation:
let your kingdom come!

In the shock of sudden illness and pain,
and in the wearing endurance
of long-term weakness,
may the Lord give peace and tranquillity,
healing and hope.

Silence

Lord of creation:
let your kingdom come!

Through the journey of death
and in the grieving of those who mourn,
may the Lord gather us up into the everlasting arms of love
and comfort us,
and bring us to life in all its fullness.

Silence

Lord of creation:
let your kingdom come!

We pray with Mary
who was full of peace and trust:
Hail, Mary . . .

In the silence of God's attentive love,
we pray our private petitions.

Silence

Celebrant
Father, in confidence we pray,
and ask you to accept these prayers,
through Jesus Christ.
Amen.

Ninth Sunday of the Year

*Wise listeners build their lives up on
the strong rock of the word of God.*

Celebrant
As the community of God's people,
let us focus our attention and still our bodies to pray.

Reader
We have heard the words and the challenge
to build our lives wisely on the bedrock of faith;
may all of us who profess to be Christians
act on what we have heard.
May the Lord bless and inspire all who preach and teach the faith
and make our worship pure and holy.

Silence

Lord God of wisdom:
you give us the word of life.

We are conscious of the double standards
and inconsistencies in our world,
and ask for hearts to be opened to hear
and recognise the wisdom of the law of love.
We ask the Lord to strengthen
and encourage each attempt
to govern with his principles,
and deal justly with his sense of mercy.

Silence

Lord God of wisdom:
you give us the word of life.

We want to take more seriously
our community commitment to our children.
May the Lord show us what needs to be started,
developed or changed
in our attitudes to one another,
and in the way we help one another's faith to grow.

Silence

Lord God of wisdom:
you give us the word of life.

The needs and concerns of all who suffer
are our concern, through love.
May we strive to address
the imprisoning poverty and hunger
of much of our world,
and involve ourselves
in the comfort, help and healing
that we ourselves ask of the Lord.

Silence

Lord God of wisdom:
you give us the word of life.

We commend to the Father's love and mercy
those who have died to this earthly life.
We give thanks for lives well lived and love shared.
May they, and we in our turn, be brought safely to heaven.

Silence

Lord God of wisdom:
you give us the word of life.

We pray with Mary,
whose faith was based on firm foundations:
Hail, Mary . . .

In silence,
we make our private petitions to God,
who always hears our prayers in faith.

Silence

Celebrant
Loving Father,
we ask you to accept these prayers
through Christ, our Lord.
Amen.

TENTH SUNDAY OF THE YEAR

*Jesus' life of healing and compassion acts out
God's desire for mercy rather than empty sacrifice.*

Celebrant
Come, let us return to the Lord who loves us,
and pray to him now.

Reader
We pray to the God of truth
that the Church may be led into the way of truth
and an ever-deepening understanding
of God's nature and will.
We pray for our leaders and teachers and pastors;
we pray for right priorities
and a softening of the ground of our hearts.

Silence

Come:
let us return to the Lord.

We pray to the God of power
for those with authority,
influence and power in our world;
for all who are easily led,
often against their conscience;
we pray for a re-aligning of right values
and a reawakening of mutual respect and trust.

Silence

Come:
let us return to the Lord.

We pray that the God of loving kindness
may watch over our homes and families,
our friends and neighbours;
we pray too for those who wish us harm
and those we find it difficult to love.

Silence

Come:
let us return to the Lord.

We bring to the God of mercy and compassion
all those who, through illness,
accident, age, abuse or human weakness
are suffering as we gather here.
May he gather them up into his love
and give his healing, strength and courage,
his hope and wholeness.
We make ourselves available as channels of his love.

Silence

Come:
let us return to the Lord.

We pray that the God of eternity,
in whom there is no beginning or end,
may welcome into his presence those who have died,
and give comfort to those
who miss their earthly company.
May he give us all a greater understanding
of the new life he offers.

Silence

Come:
let us return to the Lord.

We pray with Mary,
Mother of Mercy:
Hail, Mary . . .

Trusting in God's loving mercy,
we pray in silence
for our own cares and concerns.

Silence

Celebrant
Father of mercy,
we rejoice at your welcoming forgiveness,
and ask you to accept our prayers
through Jesus Christ.
Amen.

ELEVENTH SUNDAY OF THE YEAR

*Jesus sends his ambassadors out to proclaim
God's kingdom and bring hope and peace of mind
to the harassed and lost in every age.*

Celebrant
Let us join in praying together with all God's people
to the Lord of the harvest.

Reader
We thank the Lord for the gift of life,
and above all for his love in dying for us
who so often act as his enemies.
May he break down any barriers
which prevent us from being at peace with him,
and fill his Church with love for all
who do not yet know his peace.

Silence

You, O Lord:
you are our hope and joy.

We thank the Lord for the diversity
and richness of our world,
for the natural goodness of many,
and the innocence of the very young.
We pray for all victims of our world's mistakes and evils,
and ask for guidance and courage for our leaders and advisers.

Silence

You, O Lord:
you are our hope and joy.

We thank the Lord for the joy
of our families and friendships,
and the opportunities provided in our homes
for learning what real loving is all about.
We pray for those we love and worry about,
and those who love and worry about us,
commending one another to his keeping.

Silence

You, O Lord:
you are our hope and joy.

We thank the Lord for all the medical research
that has brought healing and quality of life to so many.
We pray for all who work in our hospitals,
hospices and clinics, and for all the patients in their care.
We pray for all who are harassed and worried,
and long for the peace of mind that eludes them.

Silence

You, O Lord:
you are our hope and joy.

We thank the Lord for all who have lived his praise
and worked for the coming of his kingdom.
May he receive into the joy of heaven all who have died in faith,
whose strong hope in the eternal God is not disappointed, but fulfilled.

Silence

You, O Lord:
you are our hope and joy.

We thank the Lord for all who sense his calling
and respond to it with joy.
We pray for still more workers in the harvest,
to gather in many to share the joy of peace.

Silence

You, O Lord:
you are our hope and joy.

We pray with Mary,
whose gift to the world was the Good Shepherd:
Hail, Mary . . .

In a time of silence,
we share with God our Father
our personal burdens, joys and sorrows.

Silence

Celebrant
Father, we ask you to hear these prayers,
through Jesus Christ,
our Saviour and our brother.
Amen.

Twelfth Sunday of the Year

*When we are willing to take up our cross with Jesus
we will also know his risen life.*

Celebrant
Let us focus our bodies, minds, hearts and wills
as we pray to the God of all creation.

Reader
The focus of our love and worship is Jesus Christ,
who alone is the Lord
and who has made us and rescued us.
May we not return to the slavery of sin
but live in freedom, serving him with joy,
in thankfulness for all he has done for us.

Silence

Heal us, Lord:
and use us to your glory.

Though the world may often reject him,
God our Father never fails to believe in us all
and love us with tenderness.
We pray for all areas of conflict, deceit,
mismanagement and greed,
and for all who are drawn into the chaos of evil.

Silence

Heal us, Lord:
and use us to your glory.

Our daily lives provide such rich ground
for acts of loving kindness,
self-discipline and courage.
May the Lord remind us of the opportunities,
and strengthen us to use them.

Silence

Heal us, Lord:
and use us to your glory.

We give thanks for all
who lovingly look after those in nursing homes,
hospitals, nurseries and prisons,
and we pray for all who need such care
and rely on others' help.

Silence

Heal us, Lord:
and use us to your glory.

We call to mind those who have recently died
and thank the Lord
for each act of goodness in their lives.
May he have mercy on them and forgive their failings,
so that they may share the joy of heaven for ever.

Silence

Heal us, Lord:
and use us to your glory.

Even when her Son was on the cross,
Mary put her trust in him.
With her we pray:
Hail, Mary . . .

Knowing that God loves us
with full understanding,
we make our private petitions to him
in silence.

Silence

Celebrant
Merciful Father, protect us during this week
and through all our lives,
and hear these prayers
which we make through Christ our Lord.
Amen.

THIRTEENTH SUNDAY OF THE YEAR

*As Christ's people we are no longer slaves to sin,
but available for righteousness.*

Celebrant
Let us pray to our heavenly Father,
who is familiar with our world
and understands our humanity.

Reader
Wherever Christians are ridiculed
or persecuted for their faith,
we ask for courage and inner strength;
wherever we are called to be witnesses,
we ask for the grace to communicate love.
Wherever love for the Lord has grown cold
we ask him to fan the flames again.

Silence

In Christ we can be dead to sin:
and alive to God.

Wherever the human spirit
is ground down by oppression,
and wherever our silence allows injustice
and corruption to flourish,
we ask for deeper compassion and commitment;
we ask for our kingdoms to become God's kingdoms,
and the desires of his heart to be ours.

Silence

In Christ we can be dead to sin:
and alive to God.

Wherever families are struggling to stay together,
and wherever there are ongoing arguments
and family feuds,
we ask for tranquillity and harmony.
Wherever children are unwanted and unloved,
neglected or in danger,
we ask the Lord for his protection and help.

Silence

In Christ we can be dead to sin:
and alive to God.

Wherever bodies, minds or spirits
are wracked with pain,
or too weak or exhausted to pray,
we ask the bathing love of God's presence,
and the practical caring
of hands working in his name.
Wherever there are doubts and the battle is strong,
we ask for his empowering and clear guidance.

Silence

In Christ we can be dead to sin:
and alive to God.

Wherever the dying are anxious and afraid,
we ask for peace;
wherever the faithful have passed
from this life into eternity,
we commend them to the unchanging
and everlasting love of the Father.

Silence

In Christ we can be dead to sin:
and alive to God.

As we join our prayers with those of Mary,
may we learn from her responsive love:
Hail, Mary . . .

Together in silence,
we name those known to us
who need our prayers.

Silence

Celebrant
Almighty God,
accept the prayers we bring you here,
through Christ our Lord.
Amen.

Fourteenth Sunday of the Year

To all who are weary with carrying heavy burdens in life,
Jesus offers rest for our souls and unthreatening relief.

Celebrant
Our loving God is here,
attentive to his children.
Let us pray to him now.

Reader
We pray that the Church
may always be open to receive the Father's love;
may we be swept clear of pomposity,
complacency or self-righteousness;
may we come humbly and simply
into his presence and wait on him,
knowing our dependence on him, and rejoicing in it.

Silence

As you have called us:
Lord, we come to you.

We pray for all world leaders and their governments;
for the strength of authority
comes not through force and domination
but through co-operation and mutual respect;
we pray for greater consideration
of the needs of one another and of our planet,
and a desire to right past wrongs and injustices.

Silence

As you have called us:
Lord, we come to you.

We pray for a growing maturity
in our thinking and our loving
that enables us to be childlike;
we pray for healing from all the damage
that prevents us from growing up;
we pray that our children in this church

may be helped to grow strong,
and we give thanks for all we learn from them.

Silence

As you have called us:
Lord, we come to you.

We pray for all who cry out for rest and relief,
all who are carrying terrible burdens that weigh them down,
all whose poverty denies them the chance of healing,
all whose wealth denies them
the chance of knowing their need of the Father's love.

Silence

As you have called us:
Lord, we come to you.

We pray for those
who die unprepared to meet the Lord,
and for all who have died recently,
both those well known to us
and those dying unknown and unnoticed
all over the world.

Silence

As you have called us:
Lord, we come to you.

We pray with Mary,
who feels for us in our weariness:
Hail, Mary . . .

In silence now,
we bring our particular petitions
to our loving Father.

Silence

Celebrant
Heavenly Father,
we rejoice in your abundant love for us,
and ask you to hear our prayers,
through Christ our Lord.
Amen.

FIFTEENTH SUNDAY OF THE YEAR

Seed of God's word, sown in good soil,
watered by his rain and warmed by his sunlight,
produces a good crop of spiritual fruit.

Celebrant
Gathered together as the people of God,
and attentive to his will, let us pray.

Reader
May the words of truth
take root in our hearts and grow to rich maturity.
May we hear the Father's will for us and act upon it;
may we take seriously our responsibility
to encourage and nurture one another in faith
at every age and every stage.

Silence

Eternal truth, living God:
your word is life and strength.

May every act of selfless giving
and every search for truth
be richly blessed and rewarded;
May assumptions be disturbed,
leading many to ponder more deeply
the spiritual dimension of their lives.
May the word of God reach all
who are ready to receive it,
and let us set no boundaries here
as to who they might be.

Silence

Eternal truth, living God:
your word is life and strength.

May the heavenly Father make our homes
places of love and growth,
welcoming to all who visit them,
and accepting and forgiving
to all who are nurtured there.

May he help us through the quarrels and heartaches
and remind us to honour one another
as his cherished ones.

Silence

Eternal truth, living God:
your word is life and strength.

May all whose bodies, souls or minds are aching
know the comforting and strengthening power
of companionship with the Lord
and the healing work of his love.
May we be more ready to support
and befriend one another through the difficult times,
in the name and love of the God we worship.

Silence

Eternal truth, living God:
your word is life and strength.

We pray for all who are making the journey
through physical death,
as they put down earthly things
and wake to the presence of the Father.
May he bring us all to share with them his life in all its fullness.

Silence

Eternal truth, living God:
your word is life and strength.

We pray with Mary,
whose faith grew abundantly:
Hail, Mary ...

In the silence of a living faith,
we pray for our own needs and cares.

Silence

Celebrant
Merciful Father,
we thank you for providing for us
and for blessing us so richly,
and ask you to accept our prayers,
through Jesus Christ.
Amen.

SIXTEENTH SUNDAY OF THE YEAR

*God's justice is always blended with mercy
and loving kindness, so that we have real hope.*

Celebrant
Let us draw near to the just and merciful God,
and pour out our concerns
for the Church and for the world.

Reader
As we join the unending cycle of prayer on our planet,
turning through time and space,
we rejoice in the upholding,
the mercy and forgiveness of our heavenly Father.
In all our small-mindedness we ask for his inbreathing,
so that we learn to look with his vision
and act with his wideness of compassion.

Silence

God of mercy:
hear us as we pray.

May the Lord our God
be present at all meetings and negotiations,
where feelings run high,
and many lives are profoundly affected
by the decisions made.
We pray for real communication
which listens to needs and appreciates difficulties,
so that we may live on this earth together
in harmony and peace.

Silence

God of mercy:
hear us as we pray.

We pray for this neighbourhood
and the particular problems it has;
for communities split apart by conflict
or crushed by tragedy.
We pray for those involved with court proceedings;

may our judicial system uphold the principle
of justice with mercy.

Silence

God of mercy:
hear us as we pray.

We pray for those who have a raw deal in this life;
for those with ongoing health problems,
and all who are caught up in war and deprivation.
We pray for a just and realistic
sharing of our resources,
and courage, support and healing for all who suffer.

Silence

God of mercy:
hear us as we pray.

We pray for those who have died
and now see their lives as they really are;
we pray that the Father may have mercy on them,
and we thank him for all their acts
of goodness and love.

Silence

God of mercy:
hear us as we pray.

We pray with Mary
who was filled with the Holy Spirit:
Hail, Mary . . .

God our Father knows our needs;
let us pray to him now
for our own intentions.

Silence

Celebrant
Father, in thankful love
we ask you to hear our prayers,
through Christ our Lord.
Amen.

Seventeenth Sunday of the Year

Jesus, the teacher, enables the ordinary,
unlearned people to understand God's wisdom –
the eternal laws of his Father's kingdom.

Celebrant
May the Spirit pray through us
as we try to put into words the longings of our hearts
for the Church and for the world.

Reader
We give thanks to the Father
for all who have helped us to pray
and to grasp something of his great love and power.
We ask his blessing and empowering
for all who teach and minister in his name;
we ask for our worship to be an overflowing
of our daily walk with him,
an expression of our deepening love.

Silence

Lord of all creation:
teach us your ways.

We give thanks for the beauty and diversity
of the created world we inhabit.
We ask for the wisdom to tend it carefully,
respecting the natural laws and sharing the resources,
listening to the weak as well as the strident,
the poor as well as the affluent and powerful.

Silence

Lord of all creation:
teach us your ways.

We give thanks
for the candour and innocence of the very young,
and for the joy of friendship;
for all with whom we share our daily life,
and those we love but seldom meet.
We ask for hearts that are skilled in listening,

so that we discern and respond to the real agendas,
and remember that a conversation
is a two-way event.

Silence

Lord of all creation:
teach us your ways.

We give thanks
for the advances in medical knowledge
and the hope of new treatments for many diseases.
We pray for all in medical research
and all whose lives are crippled or disadvantaged
by illness, frailty or damage.
May the Lord give them comfort and reassurance,
healing, wholeness and peace.

Silence

Lord of all creation:
teach us your ways.

We call to mind all those we have known and loved
who lived among us and now have died.
We pray for all who made that journey unnoticed and alone.
We ask that they may all know mercy
and the everlasting peace and joy of heaven.

Silence

Lord of all creation:
teach us your ways.

We join our prayers with those of Mary,
whose wisdom knew no bounds:
Hail, Mary . . .

Trusting in God's loving understanding,
we pray in silence, now,
for our own particular needs and concerns.

Silence

Celebrant
Father, we rejoice in the treasure of your love,
and ask you to hear our prayers,
which we make through Christ our Lord.
Amen.

EIGHTEENTH SUNDAY OF THE YEAR

God feeds all who come to him hungry, and we,
as the Church, are expected to share in that work.

Celebrant
We have gathered here
to meet with our God in worship.
Let us pray to him now.

Reader
May the Lord awaken in us our need of him
and make us hungry and thirsty for him,
both as individuals and as the Church of God.
Let no other issues side-track us from seeking him,
and may he increase our love and compassion
so that we long to serve out his love
to the world around us.

Silence

Bread of heaven:
on you we feed.

May the Lord allow our world to see the true value of things,
so that the worthless and dangerous is unmasked
and real needs acknowledged.
May he guide our leaders in wisdom and integrity,
and enable us all to co-operate in proper care
and stewardship of the world's resources.

Silence

Bread of heaven:
on you we feed.

As we eat our food this week,
may the Lord remind us of his spiritual feeding.
May the meals we prepare and eat together
be opportunities for drawing closer
to one another and to him.

Silence

Bread of heaven:
on you we feed.

We pray for all who need medical treatment
or are waiting in pain for surgery.
We pray for those who have become addicted
and long to be set free.
We pray for all whose wrong choices
have ended in heartache, disillusion and despair.

Silence

Bread of heaven:
on you we feed.

May the Lord welcome into eternity
all who have spent their lives coming to him
and now come to be with him for ever.
May he have mercy on all those approaching death
who do not know him
but reject what they imagine him to be.
May they respond to the true and living God
and know his love for ever.

Silence

Bread of heaven:
on you we feed.

With Mary, who mothered the Son of God,
we make our prayer:
Hail, Mary . . .

In the silence of our hearts,
we pray to our heavenly Father
about our own particular concerns.

Silence

Celebrant
Father of mercy,
you are always more ready to give
than we are to receive;
in thankfulness we welcome your Spirit
into our lives,
and ask you to accept our prayers,
through Jesus Christ, your Son.
Amen.

NINETEENTH SUNDAY OF THE YEAR

God is faithful to us through all the storms of life,
yet our faith in God is so very small.

Celebrant
Trusting in our faithful God, let us pray.

Reader
We pray for the gift of deeper faith in God,
so that we trust him in a way
that alters our dependence on everything else,
and allows us clearer vision
as to the direction and role of the Church.
May he remind us that it is his Church, and not ours;
his work, his power and his kingdom.

Silence

Lord our God:
let only your will be done.

As we call to mind the stormy areas of our world,
the raging and the insecurity,
the confusion and bewilderment,
the restlessness and fear,
may the calming and reassuring presence of the Lord
be sensed and recognised,
bringing peace and goodness,
righteousness and hope.

Silence

Lord our God:
let only your will be done.

May the Lord come to us in the storms of life,
when we let one another down,
mishandle opportunities
and come to the end of our strength or patience;
may he bless us with his faithful love.

Silence

Lord our God:
let only your will be done.

We place into the loving keeping of the faithful God
all those who have died,
knowing their dependence on him
and his limitless mercy.
We thank him for them and their gifts to the world,
and ask that we may, in our turn,
come to him across the waters of death
and live in his company for ever.

Silence

Lord our God:
let only your will be done.

We pray with Mary,
who listened with all her heart:
Hail, Mary . . .

As God's stillness fills our hearts,
we name any we know
who especially need our prayers.

Silence

Celebrant
Merciful Father,
hear us as we pray,
through Christ our Lord.
Amen.

TWENTIETH SUNDAY OF THE YEAR

*The good news of salvation is not limited to a
particular group or nation but available for the whole world.*

Celebrant
In faith let us pray to the God
who is Lord of all the earth.

Reader
May the worship of the Church throughout the world
be attentive and expectant,
ready to be set on fire again and again
with the outrageous foolishness of loving,
without exceptions and without limits.

Silence

Servant God:
let us honour you with our lives.

May all that encourages people
in goodness, honesty and compassion be blessed and grow;
may all that encourages self-seeking and cruelty,
prejudice and deceit wither and be exposed for its futility.
May we learn from one another's cultures
and respect one another's differences.

Silence

Servant God:
let us honour you with our lives.

We give thanks for the joy of human love,
and for all those among whom we live and work.
We pray particularly for loved ones who worry us with their health,
or circumstances, or life direction.
We pray for those among our friends and families
who do not know the Lord,
or whose faith has been shaken.

Silence

Servant God:
let us honour you with our lives.

We pray for all whose backgrounds
make belief in a loving God difficult.
We pray for all who suffer mental or emotional anguish
and those who despair.
We pray for those facing another day of pain,
another day of hunger, another day of fear.

Silence

Servant God:
let us honour you with our lives.

May all who have come to the end of this earthly life
be gathered into the eternal kingdom
and rejoice to see the Father as he really is.
We remember all whom we love but can no longer see,
and give thanks for the Father's overarching love
and undergirding faithfulness to us.

Silence

Servant God:
let us honour you with our lives.

We remember with gratitude all who gave up so much
to bring the good news to our country,
and pray that with us it may continue to be spread
until the whole earth knows the Lord's truth and love.

Silence

Servant God:
let us honour you with our lives.

We make our prayer with Mary,
faithful Mother of Jesus:
Hail, Mary . . .

Upheld by God's peace,
we pray now in silence
for any who especially need our prayers.

Silence

Celebrant
Father, we trust in your unswerving love,
and bring you these prayers,
through Jesus, our Saviour.
Amen.

TWENTY-FIRST
SUNDAY OF THE YEAR

The Church is the Body of Christ,
built on strong rock of faith and energised
by the living Breath of God.

Celebrant
Gathered as the Church of God,
members of the Body of Christ,
let us pray together.

Reader
May the Church be filled
with life and energy, spiritual health and vitality.
As we feed on the Lord, may we grow more like him;
may we exercise his loving,
minister with his tenderness,
serve with his humility
and co-operate with his vision.

Silence

In you, O Lord:
is all meaning and truth.

May the world be filled
with wonder at creation,
recognition of our mutual human responsibility,
desire for reforming what is at fault,
and hope in the possibilities of living at peace
with God and with one another.

Silence

In you, O Lord:
is all meaning and truth.

May our homes and neighbourhoods be filled
with the generosity and trust that allows space
but is always ready to encourage and support.
May we cherish our bodies, minds and spirits

as temples containing the Spirit,
and honour one another as people of God's making.

Silence

In you, O Lord:
is all meaning and truth.

We pray for all who are ill at home or in hospital,
for all in emergency surgery or in casualty;
for those who have just discovered
that they have injuries or illnesses
that will change their lives.
We pray for the work of all who heal and comfort,
all who visit the sick and counsel the distressed.

Silence

In you, O Lord:
is all meaning and truth.

We pray for the dying and those who love them;
we pray for those who have completed this life
and have made the journey through death.
We pray for the work of those
who comfort the bereaved.

Silence

In you, O Lord:
is all meaning and truth.

We pray with Mary,
Mother of the Church:
Hail, Mary . . .

We pray in silence, now,
for our own particular needs and concerns.

Silence

Celebrant
Heavenly Father,
we want to fix our lives
on your unending love,
and we ask you to accept this prayer,
Which we make through Christ our Lord.
Amen.

TWENTY-SECOND SUNDAY OF THE YEAR

As Jesus prepares for the necessary suffering of the cross,
he is tempted, through well-meaning friendship, to avoid it.

Celebrant
As followers of Jesus Christ,
let us pray to our loving Father in heaven.

Reader
We pray that the Lord may help us all in the Church
to understand what it really means
to love and serve him.
At the times of testing, may he strengthen us,
at unexpected or undeserved suffering, may he support us,
at the end of our energy, may he revive us
and teach us through it all
the inexplicable peace and joy
that comes from doing his will.

Silence

We look to the cross:
and see your love for us.

We pray that the Lord may have mercy on us
for the misdirected use of time, money and resources in this world.
In the struggle against evil and sin, may he empower us,
so that justice and righteousness are established,
upheld and celebrated,
as hearts rejoice in the freedom of all that is good.

Silence

We look to the cross:
and see your love for us.

We pray that the Lord may renew our commitment to his loving
in all our relationships, our work and our prayer.
In the hard choices, may he give us wisdom,
in the painful decisions, may he affirm us,

and may our words speak his truth,
whether that is to encourage,
to comfort or to challenge.

Silence

We look to the cross:
and see your love for us.

We pray that the Lord may bring healing and wholeness
to those who suffer, in body, mind or spirit.
In the sleepless nights and endless days of pain,
may he give the grace to persevere with patience,
and turn these dark times
into places of spiritual growth.

Silence

We look to the cross:
and see your love for us.

We pray that those who have died
may rest in the eternal peace of God's presence,
their burdens laid down and their suffering ended.

Silence

We look to the cross:
and see your love for us.

Mindful of Mary's quiet acceptance of God's will,
we join our prayers with hers:
Hail, Mary . . .

We pray our private petitions now
in the silence of God's attentive love.

Silence

Celebrant
Father, we thank you
for your constant loving provision for us,
and want to become better able to do your will;
please hear our prayers,
through the pleading of Jesus, your chosen one.
Amen.

TWENTY-THIRD SUNDAY OF THE YEAR

*It is our responsibility to encourage and uphold
one another in living by the standard of real love.*

Celebrant
In our need and human weakness,
let us come to Almighty God with our prayers.

Reader
May the unchanging God change us from the heart
until the whole Church awakens to his love
that reaches out, nurtures and celebrates,
neither holding back from what is difficult,
nor rushing in where angels fear to tread.
We pray for sensitivity and courage.

Silence

Lord, take us by the hand:
and lead us.

May the almighty God give us such love for the world
that we may pray with longing and desire,
'Your kingdom come.'
May he give our leaders the grace to see
their work as service and their role as stewards;
and sharpen both the recognition of needs
and the commitment to just provision.

Silence

Lord, take us by the hand:
and lead us.

May the merciful God
break all habits of destructive behaviour
in our homes and families, our friendships
and in all the homes of this parish.
May he develop our ability to celebrate what is good
and face what is not with honesty.

Silence

Lord, take us by the hand:
and lead us.

May the healing God lay his hands on those who suffer,
so that they may know the support of his presence
and find wholeness and peace in his love.
We pray especially for those who are locked
into the conviction
that they are beyond his forgiveness.
May they quickly discover
the freedom of his acceptance.

Silence

Lord, take us by the hand:
and lead us.

May the eternal God, in his unchanging love,
receive all those who have died in faith,
that they may rejoice in him for ever.

Silence

Lord, take us by the hand:
and lead us.

We make our prayer with Mary,
the Mother of our Redeemer:
Hail, Mary . . .

In silence,
as God our Father listens with love,
we name our own particular cares and concerns.

Silence

Celebrant
Father, we ask you to gather up
these prayers of your people,
through the merits of Jesus, our Saviour.
Amen.

TWENTY-FOURTH SUNDAY OF THE YEAR

Forgiving is a natural result of loving,
so it is not an option for us but a command.

Celebrant
In the knowledge of all God has done for us,
let us bring to him our concerns
for the Church and for the world.

Reader
We give thanks to the Father
for the love which forgives again and again,
and is prepared to trust us
with the care of his people
even after we have let him down many times.
May he teach us to minister to one another's needs
with compassion, sensitivity and discipline,
so that all are affirmed and encouraged.

Silence

The Lord is full of compassion:
his love lasts for ever.

We give thanks to the Father for the order and variety,
simplicity and complexity of this universe.
In gratitude for all that humankind is able to do,
we ask that all these gifts be used wisely and well,
for the good of all, including those as yet unborn.

Silence

The Lord is full of compassion:
his love lasts for ever.

We give thanks to the Father for what we have been forgiven
and for the opportunities we have each day
to learn the joy of forgiving others.
May he smash through our self-righteousness
and keep us learning in humility at his feet.

Silence

The Lord is full of compassion:
his love lasts for ever.

We give thanks to the Father for all those who care for the sick,
the unstable, the ungrateful and the difficult.
We pray for all who are on the receiving end
of hate, deceit, suspicion or abuse,
and for those who cause others pain
and distress of any kind.
We pray for healing and transforming.

Silence

The Lord is full of compassion:
his love lasts for ever.

We give thanks to the Father for those whose living and dying
have taught us much about love.
Freed from their pain and restrictions of age or injury,
may they enjoy for ever the life of heaven.

Silence

The Lord is full of compassion:
his love lasts for ever.

With Mary, the Mother of our merciful Lord,
we make our prayer:
Hail, Mary . . .

Now, in the space of silence,
we bring to God, our forgiving Father,
our private petitions.

Silence

Celebrant
Heavenly Father,
we know that in you we shall be safe;
give us courage to do your will gladly,
and hear our prayers in mercy,
through Christ, our Lord.
Amen.

TWENTY-FIFTH
SUNDAY OF THE YEAR

*We have no right to be envious at the
generosity and mercy God shows to others.*

Celebrant
Let us come with openness to express our concerns
for the Church and the world,
to the God of compassion and gracious understanding.

Reader
Whenever we start to get offended
by the Father's generosity or open-mindedness,
may he give us the grace to repent and join his rejoicing.
May he guard the Church against self-righteousness
and all rules and limits which he would not own,
but keep always before us the rule of love.

Silence

Not our will:
but your will, Lord, be done.

May the Lord increase in us love
not only for the victims but for the perpetrators
of evil and violence in our world;
for all governments which run on corruption and fear.
We pray for a change of heart and attitude,
an awakening to a better way of living,
and the courage to reject wrong principles.

Silence

Not our will:
but your will, Lord, be done.

May our closeness to family and friends
make us never exclusive, shutting others out,
but always inclusive, welcoming others in.
May the Lord encourage us in outgoing hospitality
and keep us from becoming possessive with those we love.

Silence

Not our will:
but your will, Lord, be done.

We pray for all offenders in prison,
that on release they will not re-offend
but find enough support to start a new life in the community.
We pray for all who are vulnerable
and unable to cope with the demands of life,
for alcoholics, drug addicts and all who are sick in mind.
We pray for proper, compassionate help for them.

Silence

Not our will:
but your will, Lord, be done.

We pray for those who have died alone,
unmourned and unnoticed.
We pray for those who have committed suicide
or died in accidents of their own making.
We commend them to the merciful love of our heavenly Father.

Silence

Not our will:
but your will, Lord, be done.

We make our prayer with Mary,
who was always open to God's will:
Hail, Mary . . .

In silence, now,
we approach our loving Father
with our private petitions.

Silence

Celebrant
Merciful Father,
you alone give meaning to our lives;
help us live in closer communion with you,
and accept these prayers,
through Jesus Christ.
Amen.

Twenty-sixth Sunday of the Year

God longs for us to die to sin and live,
but it has to be our choice, too.

Celebrant
God has called us;
as we gather in his name
let us bring to him our prayers
which come from our love and concern.

Reader
We give thanks
for all the help and encouragement
we are given from the Church –
from its worship, teaching and fellowship;
from its faithfulness in prayer.
May the Lord bless and further all loving ministry
in word and sacrament
throughout the world Church,
and inspire us all to want his will and to do it.

Silence

O God, work in us:
inspiring both will and deed.

We pray for the world,
where the misery and tragedy of wrong choices
grieves the Father's heart of love.
May there be wisdom and compassion
in all negotiations and decisions;
May there be humility in leadership
and responsibility for right action shared by all.

Silence

O God, work in us:
inspiring both will and deed.

We bring to the Lord the joys and worries,
the frustrations and accomplishments of this week
in the lives we have met and shared.

As we pray, may his light shine into all these lives
for fresh directing and lasting good.

Silence

O God, work in us:
inspiring both will and deed.

We bring to the Lord those we know
who are ill or suffering in any way.
May he give them healing, restore them
in body, mind and spirit,
and provide them with his indwelling.

Silence

O God, work in us:
inspiring both will and deed.

We remember all those who have died,
and particularly those we have known and loved.
We thank the Lord for them,
and thank him for his promise
of eternal life and peace.
May we comfort one another through his love.

Silence

O God, work in us:
inspiring both will and deed.

As we join our prayers with those of Mary,
may we learn from her example
of true humility:
Hail, Mary . . .

Let us whisper to our heavenly Father
our particular burdens of prayer.

Silence

Celebrant
Father, in you we hope and place our trust;
please accept these prayers,
and help us to do your will,
through Christ Jesus.
Amen.

Twenty-seventh Sunday of the Year

God does everything possible for our spiritual growth
and well-being, but still we can choose hostility and rejection.

Celebrant
Let us pray trustfully to the God
who has loved us into being
and cherished us all our life.

Reader
As he guides his Church
into ways of spiritual beauty and gracious wisdom,
may the word of the Lord be spoken out with passion
and heard with humility and joy.
May he sustain and feed us so that we bear fruit in abundance.

Silence

Root your people:
firmly in your love.

May justice and righteousness
flourish in this neighbourhood, this country, this world.
May the Lord bless those who work to right what is wrong
and mediate where there is conflict.
We ask him to raise up leaders who are happy to serve
and to protect them from power's corruption.

Silence

Root your people:
firmly in your love.

We thank the Lord
for the nurturing we have received,
and pray for our children and young people as they grow.
May the Lord protect them from evil and strengthen them in faith;
may they continue to be his for ever.

Silence

Root your people:
firmly in your love.

We pray for comfort and healing for all
who are in any kind of need, sorrow or pain.
May they sense the reassuring presence of the Lord
and know that he is there with them,
wherever their journey takes them.

Silence

Root your people:
firmly in your love.

We pray for those who have died to this earthly life,
and now see the Lord face to face.
We remember his mercy and commit our loved ones
to the safety of his keeping.

Silence

Root your people:
firmly in your love.

We thank the Lord for all the care
and attention that he lavishes on us;
may he make us worthy of our calling
and continue his ongoing work in us.

Silence

Root your people:
firmly in your love.

With Mary, who so calmly
made herself available to God's will,
we join our prayer:
Hail, Mary . . .

Now, in the space of silence,
we bring our private petitions
to the Lord of the vineyard.

Silence

Celebrant
Father, we thank you for your steadfast love,
and ask you to accept these prayers,
through Christ our Lord.
Amen.

TWENTY-EIGHTH SUNDAY OF THE YEAR

We are all invited to God's wedding banquet,
but in accepting we must allow the rags of our old life
to be exchanged for the freely given robes of holiness and right living.

Celebrant
Invited by our God, we have gathered here.
Let us now voice our prayers
for the Church and for the world.

Reader
When either the traditional or the progressive
blinds us to the truth of the Father's will,
may he clear our vision and speak through our prejudices
until we are once again open to his changing.
May we be, before anything else, his people,
sharing his concerns and desires.

Silence

As you have called us:
Lord, we come.

We recognise how powerful
the influences are in our world
which distract many and lead away from the truth.
We pray for the quiet whisper of wisdom
to be noticed and acknowledged in many lives;
we pray for widespread discipline of the heart,
a new openness to generosity of spirit.

Silence

As you have called us:
Lord, we come.

May our homes and daily schedules
be part of the territory of the kingdom,
where it is God's will which guides
and his love which rules.

Silence

As you have called us:
Lord, we come.

Our hearts rail against the cruelty
and unfairness of suffering and disease,
and we kneel now alongside all in pain
and weep with them, crying out to the Lord
for comfort and the healing of his love.
That he shares our sorrow
gives us the grace to bear it.

Silence

As you have called us:
Lord, we come.

As death takes from us those we love
and we find it hard to live without them,
we pray that we may share with them
the Father's peace over which death has no power at all.

Silence

As you have called us:
Lord, we come.

With Mary, bearer of God's Son,
we make our prayer:
Hail, Mary . . .

We pray in silence, now,
for those known to us
who have particular needs.

Silence

Celebrant
Lord, in thankfulness
for all your rich blessings to us every day,
we offer you our prayers,
through Christ our Saviour.
Amen.

TWENTY-NINTH
SUNDAY OF THE YEAR

*All leaders and rulers are subject to the ultimate authority
and power of God, the living truth.*

Celebrant
Let us focus our gaze
on the great God of our making,
as we pour out to him our prayers.

Reader
We pray that the Church
may have such maturity and wisdom
that we may not be swayed
from our purpose and calling
by trivialities or worldly pressures,
but know increasingly
our dependence on the Lord in all things
and proclaim his Gospel
with steadfastness and joy.

Silence

You, O Lord:
are the ground of our being.

May all monarchs, leaders and heads of state
be given graciousness and integrity,
that all in power and authority
may undertake their duties in a spirit of humility;
that the oppressed may find a voice,
and the nations work together
for the good of the world.

Silence

You, O Lord:
are the ground of our being.

May all our homes and places of work and leisure
know and radiate the Lord's harmony and peace;
may we have the grace to respect one another and ourselves

in the way we talk and think,
and in the way we behave.

Silence

You, O Lord:
are the ground of our being.

We pray for peace in the hearts
of all who are agitated, anxious or confused.
We pray that the Lord may lay his hands of healing on all who are ill,
that they may know his reassurance and love.

Silence

You, O Lord:
are the ground of our being.

May all who have kept faith be welcomed into the kingdom
and lay their burdens down.
May they rest in peace for ever.

Silence

You, O Lord:
are the ground of our being.

We make our prayer with Mary,
who joyfully poured out her thanks and praise:
Hail, Mary . . .

Together in silence,
we name those known to us
who need our prayers.

Silence

Celebrant
In joy, Father,
we offer you our prayers and our praise,
through Jesus Christ,
our Saviour and our brother.
Amen.

Thirtieth Sunday of the Year

We are to love God with our whole being,
and love others as much as we love ourselves.

Celebrant
In love and trust, let us pray to our God.

Reader
We pray for the courage
to tell out God's truth without fear,
and to work for his kingdom with joy.
In gratitude for the support
and love of other Christians,
and for the richness of our varied traditions,
may we focus our attention on the Lord with such love
that all unnecessary divisions between us crumble.

Silence

You are the Lord:
there is no other.

We pray for our law makers and keepers;
may our laws work to uphold what is just and true.
We pray that we may live
in godly peace and goodwill through choice,
rather than through fear of punishment;
through the desire to live well,
rather than avoiding detection.

Silence

You are the Lord:
there is no other.

In all our day-to-day living
may we reject deceit and flattery,
so that our motives and behaviour are honest,
and our love for one another clear as the day.

Silence

You are the Lord:
there is no other.

We pray for all law breakers and their families;
for those in prison
and those returning to the community.
We pray for those imprisoned by guilt or shame,
or trapped by physical frailty, illness or paralysis.
We pray for those whose lives are tragically disrupted
by war and famine, poverty and disease.

Silence

You are the Lord:
there is no other.

We remember those who, dying in faith,
rejoice to see the Lord as he is.
We give thanks for their example
and commend them to the Father's peace for ever.

Silence

You are the Lord:
there is no other.

We give thanks for the love
poured out to us each moment of each day,
and ask the grace to live our gratitude
and give freely of what we have freely received.

Silence

You are the Lord:
there is no other.

We make our prayer with Mary,
Mother of the Lord of Love:
Hail, Mary . . .

Trustingly we pray to our loving Lord,
for our own needs and cares.

Silence

Celebrant
Father, we ask you to work your love in our lives,
and accept these prayers we have brought to you,
through Christ, our Lord.
Amen.

THIRTY-FIRST SUNDAY OF THE YEAR

*Our lives need to reflect our faith;
we are not just called to tell the good news but to live it as well.*

Celebrant
Let us bare our souls before God as we pray.

Reader
We pray for those in ordained and lay ministries;
for a deepening of our own commitment to Christ,
and a cleansing of our lives,
so that the Church is a true image
of the Body of Christ.

Silence

Lord of truth:
light our way.

We pray for all who are fearful of being their true selves;
all who cannot face the truth of their sin
and dare not admit it,
either to themselves or to God.
We pray for courage,
and the humility to see ourselves as he sees us;
our actions and our motives as he sees them.

Silence

Lord of truth:
light our way.

May we learn not to take ourselves too seriously,
and come to recognise our weaknesses and failures
as well as our strengths.

Silence

Lord of truth:
light our way.

We pray for those who are going through difficult
or confused times at the moment;
those whose lives feel full of pain and darkness;
those who do not realise their need of God;
those who have rejected him through being shown
a false image of his nature.

Silence

Lord of truth:
light our way.

We pray for those who have died to this life
and now see the Father face to face.
May his merciful love surround them
in his eternity.

Silence

Lord of truth:
light our way.

Encouraged by Mary's example of integrity,
we join our prayers with hers:
Hail, Mary . . .

We name our particular prayer burdens now,
in silence filled with love.

Silence

Celebrant
Father, in your love accept our prayers,
through Christ our Saviour.
Amen.

THIRTY-SECOND SUNDAY OF THE YEAR

*We need to keep ourselves awake and prepared
so that the Day of the Lord does not come to us
as darkness rather than light.*

Celebrant
In the power of the Spirit,
let us pray to the Lord.

Reader
May the Church all over the world
be anointed with the oil of the Spirit,
so that we burn brightly,
lighting the dark world with love and truth.
May church communities be kept from error and sin,
so that, through word and sacrament,
we may be supplied with all our souls require.

Silence

Waken us, Lord:
to understand your love.

May the Spirit of the Lord
take the false values of our world and upend them;
take the oppressed and free them;
take the leaders and inspire them;
take the past and redeem it,
the present and fill it,
the future and guide us in it.

Silence

Waken us, Lord:
to understand your love.

It is in our homes and daily tasks
that the heavenly Father trains us in loving obedience.
We pray for those who have to live and work with us
and are familiar with our habits, gifts and faults.
May we make the most of the opportunities
to love, to forgive, to stand back and to reach out.

Silence

Waken us, Lord:
to understand your love.

As we pray for all who are ill
in body, mind or spirit,
may they be surrounded with love and healing,
reassurance and peace.
We pray for those
who are too weak or exhausted to pray,
but simply know they ache
for the comforting presence of the Lord.

Silence

Waken us, Lord:
to understand your love.

We commend to the Father's mercy and love
those who have died in his faith and friendship;
may we all share in the joy
of Christ's coming in glory.

Silence

Waken us, Lord:
to understand your love.

With Mary, Mother of Jesus,
let us pray:
Hail, Mary . . .

In a time of silence,
we share with God our Father
our personal burdens, joys and sorrows.

Silence

Celebrant
Father, whose character is full
of mercy and compassion,
accept these prayers
which we make through Jesus, our Saviour.
Amen.

THIRTY-THIRD SUNDAY OF THE YEAR

*The Day of the Lord will hold terror for the wicked and unprepared,
but rejoicing for those living in God's light.*

Celebrant
Gathered as God's people, let us pray.

Reader
If we presume on his mercy,
may the Lord alert us and shatter our complacency;
if we are doubting his mercy,
may he affirm in us the reality of his forgiveness.
May we, as the Church, encourage and warn,
rebuke the sin, but love the sinner.

Silence

Christ will come again:
make us ready to meet him.

May the Lord raise up prophets to speak out his truth,
and draw attention to whatever needs changing
in our world, our expectations and assumptions,
our management of resources and finances,
our systems of government and our attitudes.
May all peoples come to recognise his truth.

Silence

Christ will come again:
make us ready to meet him.

May the Lord fill our homes and places of work
with so much love that tensions and barriers melt away,
conflicts are resolved
and troubles lightened by being lovingly shared.
May hearts which had given up
be opened again to his love.

Silence

Christ will come again:
make us ready to meet him.

May all in misery and despair
turn to find the Lord close beside them in their heartache,
not condemning but loving them in their pain.
May all who are locked in terror or guilt be set free,
and may those whom long-term illness wearies
be strengthened to persevere,
freed from resentment.

Silence

Christ will come again:
make us ready to meet him.

We commend to the Father's mercy all who have died,
and thank him for that eternal healing
which frees us from all pain and suffering.

Silence

Christ will come again:
make us ready to meet him.

We thank the Lord for the gifts and talents
he has given us.
May we have the courage to use them
for the good of the world.

Silence

Christ will come again:
make us ready to meet him.

We make our prayer with Mary,
who used all her gifts in God's service:
Hail, Mary . . .

God our Father loves us:
in silence
we make our private petitions to him.

Silence

Celebrant
Heavenly Father, grant these prayers
which we bring before you,
in the name of Jesus Christ.
Amen.

CHRIST THE KING

In total humility, at one with the least of his people,
Jesus, the Messiah or Christ, reigns as King,
with full authority and honour for eternity.

Celebrant
Let us humble ourselves in the presence of God
and pray to him for the Church and for the world.

Reader
In all our ministry as the Church,
both laity and clergy,
on Sundays and on weekdays,
may we give glory to God
and further his kingdom.
May he direct us to those who are searching
and give us the wisdom to know
how best to draw them to his love.

Silence

We are your people:
the sheep of your pasture.

May we actively seek to do good,
to stand up against injustice and work for peace;
May the world be rid of the terrible evils
that result from unvoiced objections,
and unspoken misgivings.
May we have the courage to act as true citizens of heaven.

Silence

We are your people:
the sheep of your pasture.

May the ways we manage our homes,
decisions, time and money
be in keeping with our calling
as inheritors of the kingdom.
May God's love undergird all our loving.

Silence

We are your people:
the sheep of your pasture.

May the Lord help us to share his work of loving care:
to search for the lost,
to bring back those who have strayed,
to bind up the injured,
and to strengthen the weak.

Silence

We are your people:
the sheep of your pasture.

May the Lord welcome into his kingdom
all whose lives show them to be his servants,
whether or not they have known him by name.
May we all be prepared to meet him
with the confidence of sins confessed and forgiven.

Silence

We are your people:
the sheep of your pasture.

With Mary, Mother of Christ the King,
we make our prayer:
Hail, Mary . . .

We make our private petitions now,
in the knowledge that God our Father
listens with love.

Silence

Celebrant
Trusting in your great love, dear Father,
we lay our prayers before you,
and ask you to hear our requests
through Christ Jesus.
Amen.

YEAR B

First Sunday of Advent

Be alert and watchful; keep yourselves ready.

Celebrant
As we begin a new year in the life of the Church,
we pray to the God who made us.

Reader
We come to the Lord just as we are
and ask that his kingdom may come
to be within us and in this place.
We pray for an increase in faith
that we may become the lights in darkness
that we are called to be.

Silence

O God, keep us awake to you:
and alive to your call.

The signs in our world of hate, distrust and greed
are shown to us clearly every day.
May our eyes see the signs of hope and victory;
the opportunities for loving service,
for encouragement, reassurance and thanksgiving.

Silence

O God, keep us awake to you:
and alive to your call.

May the parenting and befriending
in all our relationships be blessed,
and may our love for one another be increased.
We pray for the humility
to accept guidance and warnings, lovingly given,
and the courage to uphold one another in the faith.

Silence

O God, keep us awake to you:
and alive to your call.

In love, we bring to our prayers
those who are weary
with ongoing pain and weakness,
those who are frail with age
and all who are vulnerable;
May the Lord pour his living strength into their lives
and protect them from all that is harmful.

Silence

O God, keep us awake to you:
and alive to your call.

We pray for all who have come
to the end of their earthly life,
and for those whose lives
feel empty without them.
May the Lord give comfort to the bereaved,
and everlasting peace to all who rest in his love.

Silence

O God, keep us awake to you:
and alive to your call.

With Mary, the Mother of Jesus,
let us pray:
Hail, Mary . . .

In silence, now,
we bring to God our Father
any needs and concerns
known to us personally.

Silence

Celebrant
Lord, our Creator,
we thank you for the wonder of our being,
and ask you to hear our prayers,
through Jesus Christ.
Amen.

SECOND SUNDAY OF ADVENT

*John the Baptist prepares the way
for the coming of the Messiah by helping
the people to realign their lives.*

Celebrant
As we gather expectantly in God's presence,
let us pray.

Reader
We pray that God's cleansing and liberating power
may give us the courage and perception
to see ourselves as we really are,
and lead us to true repentance.

Silence

Come, O come, Emmanuel:
come and live in us.

We pray for the world's leaders and all in authority,
that they may lead and govern wisely and honestly,
without corruption and for the common good.

Silence

Come, O come, Emmanuel:
come and live in us.

We pray that every family
may be surrounded and upheld
by God's loving presence,
that conflicts may be healed and needs provided for,
and every act of kindness blessed.

Silence

Come, O come, Emmanuel:
come and live in us.

We pray for reassurance and healing,
hope and patience
for all who are suffering in any way;

for freedom to all imprisoned by hate or guilt,
and for a change of heart to all who need to forgive.

Silence

Come, O come, Emmanuel:
come and live in us.

We pray for those
who have completed their time on earth.
May they know the freedom, joy and fullness
of unending life in heaven.

Silence

Come, O come, Emmanuel:
come and live in us.

We make our prayer with Mary,
who prepared a way for the Lord:
Hail, Mary . . .

As God's stillness fills our hearts,
we make our private petitions and thanksgivings.

Silence

Celebrant
In great thankfulness
for your compassionate love,
dear Father,
we ask you to accept our prayers,
through Jesus Christ our Lord.
Amen.

THIRD SUNDAY OF ADVENT

*In Jesus, God will be fulfilling the Messianic
prophecies about the promised Saviour.*

Celebrant
Let us pray now to the living God,
who always keeps his promises,
and who knows us so well.

Reader
May the Church always be faithful
in telling the good news, comforting the desolate,
actively loving justice,
and drawing many to freedom
through the joy of the Father's loving forgiveness.

Silence

Keep us faithful, Lord:
to your calling.

As the Church, we pray for the world,
that there may be integrity in leadership;
mercy and justice for rich and poor,
strong and weak;
that there may be peace among nations
and respect for all.

Silence

Keep us faithful, Lord:
to your calling.

As the family of believers,
we pray for those around us now and their needs;
and for the families we represent, and their needs.
May the love of Christ be shown in what we do
and how we speak and how we spend.

Silence

Keep us faithful, Lord:
to your calling.

In compassion we call to mind
all who are locked in physical or emotional pain,
all who are weighed down with worry,
guilt or despair.
May they be restored and refreshed, comforted and freed.

Silence

Keep us faithful, Lord:
to your calling.

As resurrection people,
we commend to the Father's love
those who have died to this earthly life.
May they, and we in our turn, experience for ever
the joy of eternal life.

Silence

Keep us faithful, Lord:
to your calling.

With Mary,
who mothered the Son of God,
we make our prayer:
Hail, Mary . . .

In the knowledge
that God wants our spiritual happiness,
let us pray our private petitions.

Silence

Celebrant
As part of your generous creation, Father,
we give you thanks and praise,
and ask you to accept these prayers,
through Christ Jesus.
Amen.

FOURTH SUNDAY OF ADVENT

*God's promised kingdom, announced both
to King David in ancient times and to Mary
by the angel Gabriel, will go on for ever.*

Celebrant
Gathered as the Church of God in this place,
let us pray together for the coming of the kingdom.

Reader
We pray that the Church
may be quiet enough to hear God's voice,
humble enough to move in God's way,
and excited enough to spread the good news.

Silence

Living God:
let your kingdom come.

We pray that all who lead
may do so with integrity and respect for others;
that those in positions of authority
may be blessed with humility and a sense of right;
that unjust practices may be changed for good
and conflicts of great tension be peacefully resolved.

Silence

Living God:
let your kingdom come.

May our homes be places
of loving acceptance and developing faith;
in all our friendships may we learn
to grow in generosity of spirit.

Silence

Living God:
let your kingdom come.

When the waiting is long and painful,
may all who have to wait
be given patience and courage;
may those who are wounded,
whether physically or emotionally,
be granted healing
and the assurance of God's presence.

Silence

Living God:
let your kingdom come.

May those who have died to this life,
and whose hope is in the Lord,
be welcomed into eternity.
May those who mourn them be comforted,
and their pain be touched by the divine love.

Silence

Living God:
let your kingdom come.

Remembering Mary's humble acceptance
of God's will,
we join our prayers with hers:
Hail, Mary . . .

The God of Peace is listening;
in this silence we name those we know
who are in any particular need.

Silence

Celebrant
Heavenly Father, accept our prayers,
and make us channels of your peace,
through the power of Jesus Christ.
Amen.

CHRISTMAS DAY

Jesus Christ, the world's Saviour,
is here with us, born as a human baby.

Celebrant
As we gather to celebrate Christmas,
let us pray to the living God.

Reader
With gratitude for our Church and its people,
for our deacons, priests and bishops,
and all who pray,
may we all be blessed and strengthened
in our service,
so we can touch the world with God's love.

Silence

Holy God:
be born in us today.

We are thankful for the blessings of creation,
for our world and all its beauty.
May we learn God's ways of love and truth,
that his kingdom may grow and flourish.

Silence

Holy God:
be born in us today.

We pray for God's blessing on all those we love –
our families, neighbours and friends,
whether present with us today or far away.
May we all grow closer
in the happiness of human loving and sharing.

Silence

Holy God:
be born in us today.

With gratitude for our own health and strength,
we pray now for help and healing
wherever people ache with pain and sorrow,
loneliness or fear.
May they be blessed in their need
and surrounded with love.

Silence

Holy God:
be born in us today.

We pray for those who have died
and all for whom Christmas
sharpens the loss of loved ones.

Silence

Holy God:
be born in us today.

We make our prayer with Mary,
in whom the Word was made flesh:
Hail, Mary . . .

We name in this silence
any known to us
with particular needs or burdens.

Silence

Celebrant
Father, we can never thank you enough
for coming to rescue us;
please hear our prayers which we offer
through Jesus, your Son.
Amen.

FIRST SUNDAY OF CHRISTMAS: THE HOLY FAMILY

*The Saviour of the world is born as a fully human baby
into a real human family.*

Celebrant
We are all members of God's family.
Let us pray to him now.

Reader
We pray that our church communities
may reflect the love and mutual care
shown to us in the example of the Holy Family;
that we may recognise our responsibility
to provide spiritual nurture for our young.

Silence

Come, Lord:
and live among us.

We pray for all parents and children,
that our laws and structures of society
may uphold and support them.
We pray for the very poor
and those who struggle to survive.

Silence

Come, Lord:
and live among us.

We pray for the families we know well,
especially those with conflicts or pressures;
may the Holy Spirit protect them
so that each family member
may know they are loved
and grow in love themselves.

Silence

Come, Lord:
and live among us.

We pray for all refugees and war-torn families;
for all children at risk of abuse,
and all families where there is violence.
We pray that the Spirit may bring hope,
healing and transformation.

Silence

Come, Lord:
and live among us.

We pray for those who have died
and for their families who mourn them.
May they receive a merciful judgement
and experience the unending peace of heaven.

Silence

Come, Lord:
and live among us.

We make our prayer with Mary,
Mother of the Church:
Hail, Mary . . .

As members of Christ's family,
we pray to our loving Lord,
who considers each one of us special.

Silence

Celebrant
Heavenly Father, dwell in our hearts and homes,
and accept these prayers through Jesus Christ,
our brother and Redeemer.
Amen.

SECOND SUNDAY OF CHRISTMAS

The Word made flesh at Christmas was always with God,
always expressing his creative love.

Celebrant
Let us pray to the God
who loves us enough to come and save us.

Reader
We pray for the areas of the Church
which are weak in faith,
despondent or complacent;
that we may be recharged
with the power of God's love,
reawakened to the good news,
and revitalised with the breath of the Spirit.

Silence

Living Word of God:
be spoken in our lives.

We pray for all areas of misunderstanding
between peoples and nations,
between needs and offers of help;
make us more ready to listen than instruct,
more ready to encourage than crush.

Silence

Living Word of God:
be spoken in our lives.

We pray for family feuds and difficulties
to be resolved and learnt from;
for the words we speak
to express love and respect,
with true charity and forgiveness.

Silence

Living Word of God:
be spoken in our lives.

We pray for all who have difficulty
hearing and speaking,
reading and writing;
for the oppressed and persecuted
whose voices are silenced,
and for all who have yet to hear
the good news of God's love.

Silence

Living Word of God:
be spoken in our lives.

We pray for those who have died
and those who are dying now;
may the Word of life
encourage them on their journey
and bring them safely to the eternal kingdom.

Silence

Living Word of God:
be spoken in our lives.

We join our prayers with those of Mary,
whose Son has brought us salvation:
Hail, Mary . . .

In a time of silence
we share with God our Father
any needs and burdens
known to us personally.

Silence

Celebrant
Almighty Father, hear our prayers
and make us alert to your response,
through Christ our Lord.
Amen.

THE EPIPHANY OF THE LORD

Jesus, the promised Messiah,
is shown to the Gentile world.

Celebrant
Let us pray to the God who loves us
and knows the terrain we travel.

Reader
We thank God for all those who brought
the good news of Jesus to us,
and all who nourish our faith today.
We pray that the whole people of God
may work in unity and openness
for the coming of God's kingdom.

Silence

Lord God:
we offer you ourselves.

We thank God that salvation is for all people,
and pray for a just and accepting world
where none is rejected, despised
or treated with contempt.

Silence

Lord God:
we offer you ourselves.

We thank God for the privilege of parenting
and of living in communities;
we pray that our homes and churches
may be welcoming and generous-hearted.

Silence

Lord God:
we offer you ourselves.

We thank God for all who care
with such thoughtfulness and practical loving
for those who are vulnerable,
and especially for the very young.
We pray for healing and wholeness,
peace of mind, protection and hope.

Silence

Lord God:
we offer you ourselves.

We thank God for all who have reached
the end of their earthly journey in faith,
that they may be welcomed into eternity.
May we use the time left to us here
as good stewards of God's gifts.

Silence

Lord God:
we offer you ourselves.

We make our prayer with Mary,
who showed her Son to the Wise Men:
Hail, Mary . . .

Knowing that our loving Father is listening,
we bring our personal petitions to him now.

Silence

Celebrant
In thankfulness, Father,
we offer you our lives
and our prayers,
through Jesus Christ.
Amen.

THE BAPTISM OF THE LORD

Through the Holy Spirit,
Jesus is affirmed at his Baptism as God's beloved Son,
and we too are given the Spirit of God which affirms
us as God's adopted daughters and sons.

Celebrant
Let the Spirit of God in our hearts plead
for the Church and for the world.

Reader
We pray that the Spirit
may fill the Church with such joy in believing
that all Christians overflow with love,
compassion, generosity and humility.

Silence

May the Spirit of God:
fill us to overflowing.

May God's power and justice
fill the arenas of leadership and conflict
with sharpened consciences and with courage,
so that wise decisions are made,
needs met and wrongs righted.

Silence

May the Spirit of God:
fill us to overflowing.

May God's gentleness and truth
fill every home with new insight
and greater understanding.
Break down the divisive barriers
and build up our capacity to love.

Silence

May the Spirit of God:
fill us to overflowing.

May God's attentive caring
fill us with practical compassion;
may all who suffer be heard,
comforted and cared for.
May there be healing for both their situation
and our hardness of heart.

Silence

May the Spirit of God:
fill us to overflowing.

May God's unending being
fill death with life and the dying with hope.
May we all be prepared
for life which lasts for ever.

Silence

May the Spirit of God:
fill us to overflowing.

Mary opened her life
to the loving power of God;
we now make our prayer with her:
Hail, Mary . . .

Conscious of the Holy Spirit among us,
we share with God our Father
our personal burdens, joys and sorrows.

Silence

Celebrant
Father, we rejoice
in your uncompromising love for us,
and ask you to hear our prayers,
through Jesus Christ.
Amen.

FIRST SUNDAY OF LENT

After his Baptism Jesus is led by the Spirit into the wilderness
before returning to proclaim God's kingdom.

Celebrant
As we begin this season of Lent,
let us move off into the desert
to communicate with our God.

Reader
As we come before God
with all our muddled priorities
and conflicting agendas,
we pray that we may be made whole
as the Body of Christ;
that we may have the strength to renounce evil,
and the courage to announce the kingdom of peace.

Silence

With our God:
all things are possible.

With the world's clamour ringing in our ears,
with comfort zones beckoning us,
but the pain of injustice refusing to be shut out,
we pray for the world's healing,
and for an end to all lying and deceit.

Silence

With our God:
all things are possible.

We come with the demands of home, family, work,
and expectations warring in us
for space and attention.
We pray on behalf of those
too busy or too exhausted to pray;
that our daily lives may be washed in peace,
ordered in holiness and lit up with joy.

Silence

With our God:
all things are possible.

We come with the needs and sorrows,
pain and suffering of our brothers and sisters
all over the world, who are aching –
physically, emotionally or spiritually;
we pray that they may be touched
by God's comforting and healing love.

Silence

With our God:
all things are possible.

In this Lenten season,
we come to realign our lives
in the context of eternity,
and to commend to God's love
our own loved ones
who have passed through earthly death
to the life which has no ending.

Silence

With our God:
all things are possible.

Remembering Mary's dedication and love,
we pray with her:
Hail, Mary . . .

We make our private petitions
and thanksgivings
together now in silence.

Silence

Celebrant
Father, we thank you
for showing us the way to abundant life,
and ask you to hear our prayers
through Jesus Christ.
Amen.

SECOND SUNDAY OF LENT

Christ's willingness to face suffering and death,
in order to save us, proclaims the total sacrificial love of God.

Celebrant
Let us pray to our God
whose glory fills heaven and earth.

Reader
That in focusing our lives and our worship on God
we may increasingly reflect his love and brightness
so that others are drawn to worship him.

Silence

Lord, open our eyes:
to see your glory.

That the world's leaders may be committed
to alleviating unnecessary suffering
and working co-operatively
for the good of all who inhabit this planet.

Silence

Lord, open our eyes:
to see your glory.

That every word we speak
and every meeting we arrange
may further the building of God's kingdom.

Silence

Lord, open our eyes:
to see your glory.

That all who suffer, whether physically,
spiritually, mentally or emotionally,
may know the comfort, healing
and transforming of God's love.

Silence

Lord, open our eyes:
to see your glory.

That those who have died to this earthly life
may share in the glory of heaven.

Silence

Lord, open our eyes:
to see your glory.

With Mary,
who shared her Son's sorrows,
we make our prayer:
Hail, Mary . . .

We pray in silence, now,
for our individual needs and concerns.

Silence

Celebrant
Father, whose character is always full of mercy,
hear our prayers
through the pleading of your Son, Jesus Christ.
Amen.

Third Sunday of Lent

God's wisdom may shock us. Jesus,
obedient to God's Law and fulfilling it, dies a death which,
according to the Law, makes him cursed.

Celebrant
As God has called us,
so we have come to pray.

Reader
We pray for the Church, the Body of Christ,
with all its collected gifts and weaknesses;
may we receive the grace to recognise
that in the Spirit we are one,
and curb in us all tendency to division.

Silence

May we hear you, Lord:
and want to obey.

We pray for the world
in all its beauty and richness;
may we have the desire
and the generosity of spirit
to share our planet's food and resources,
to care for its people's well-being,
and to foster peace and justice for all.

Silence

May we hear you, Lord:
and want to obey.

We pray for those we love –
those we see each day and those we miss;
may we cherish one another
as we live the loving way of your commands.

Silence

May we hear you, Lord:
and want to obey.

We pray for all victims of selfish or violent acts,
and for those whose lives are trapped in sin.
We pray for all whose bodies and minds
have difficulty functioning.
May we be more sensitive to their needs.

Silence

May we hear you, Lord:
and want to obey.

We pray for those who have died
and for those who miss their physical presence.
May the Lord have mercy on them;
may they, and we in our turn,
rest in the peace of God's enfolding love.

Silence

May we hear you, Lord:
and want to obey.

We pray with Mary,
our spiritual Mother:
Hail, Mary . . .

As God's stillness fills our hearts,
we name any we know
who especially need our prayer.

Silence

Celebrant
Father, we thank you
for giving us this opportunity to pray,
and ask you to hear us,
through Jesus Christ.
Amen.

Fourth Sunday of Lent

God loves us so much that he is generous with his mercy.

Celebrant
Trusting not in our own worthiness,
but in God's mercy,
let us pray.

Reader
We pray for all who lead worship
and teach the faith to others;
that hearts may be open to receive
the message of spiritual health and life.

Silence

Day by day, O Lord:
may we remember your love.

We pray for all world leaders,
both in their public office
and in their private lives.
We pray for a collective desire for peace
and the courage to uphold right values.

Silence

Day by day, O Lord:
may we remember your love.

We pray for those we live and work with,
that none may be taken for granted
or live in a climate of condemnation;
but that we may all encourage one another in love.

Silence

Day by day, O Lord:
may we remember your love.

We pray for all condemned to death
or long prison sentences;
for those with long-term and debilitating illness;
for all who have been damaged.

Silence

Day by day, O Lord:
may we remember your love.

We pray for those who have died
and those who miss their physical presence;
May they see the fullness of eternal life.

Silence

Day by day, O Lord:
may we remember your love.

Remembering Mary's hopefulness and love,
we make our prayer with her:
Hail, Mary . . .

We pray in silence, now,
for any who especially need our prayer.

Silence

Celebrant
Merciful Father,
you know our deepest needs;
let your will be done in our lives
and in the lives of those for whom we pray,
through Jesus Christ.
Amen.

FIFTH SUNDAY OF LENT

*Through Christ's death, full life would come
to people of all nations and generations.*

Celebrant
Let us pray to the God who loves us
and understands our needs.

Reader
We pray for all Church leaders,
teachers and pastors,
and all who are being called
into particular ministries, both lay and ordained.
We pray especially for any who are wrestling
with the demands of such a calling,
that they may be given courage
to offer themselves in the Lord's service.

Silence

Let your name be glorified:
let your will be done.

We pray for the nations of the world,
that, in all their plans and actions,
conflicts and disasters;
the Lord may guard the children,
guide the leaders
and give us all his peace.

Silence

Let your name be glorified:
let your will be done.

We pray for those
who are weighed down with suffering,
or imprisoned by their fears.
May their burdens be eased
and may they be given the strength
to bear what cannot be avoided.

Silence

Let your name be glorified:
let your will be done.

We pray that those whose earthly lives have ended
may have mercy and everlasting peace.

Silence

Let your name be glorified:
let your will be done.

With Mary,
whose heart was pierced with sorrow,
we make our prayer:
Hail, Mary . . .

We pray to our heavenly Father
about our own particular concerns.

Silence

Celebrant
Father, with thankful hearts
we offer these concerns
for the Church and for the world,
through Jesus, our Saviour.
Amen.

PALM (PASSION) SUNDAY

*As the Messiah, Jesus enters Jerusalem, knowing that he rides
towards rejection and death in order to save his people.*

Celebrant
As we face up to the costly loving
shown by our God,
let us approach him in humility
and pray to him now.

Reader
We pray that as a Church
we may love God and one another,
and go on loving,
through insult and praise,
through acceptance and rejection,
in the sure knowledge that the Lord is our God.

Silence

Make us strong:
to do your will in all things.

May the kingdoms of this world
soak up the values of God's kingdom;
may their leaders and their peoples
uphold what is right and just,
and establish a social order
which is rooted in Godly love.

Silence

Make us strong:
to do your will in all things.

In all the heartaches and joys
of human relationships,
may we be governed by selfless love,
faithful and forgiving without limit.

Silence

Make us strong:
to do your will in all things.

May all who suffer come to know
the comforting presence and healing power
of God's forgiving love.

Silence

Make us strong:
to do your will in all things.

We pray for all
who are making that last journey of death,
that they may be surrounded with God's peace
and rest in his love for ever.

Silence

Make us strong:
to do your will in all things.

We join our prayers with those of Mary,
Mother of the King of love:
Hail, Mary . . .

Upheld by God's peace,
we pray now in silence
for any needs known to us personally.

Silence

Celebrant
Father, we rejoice
in your companionship and loyalty,
and ask you to hear our prayers,
for the sake of Jesus, our Saviour.
Amen.

EASTER DAY

Jesus is alive; God's love has won
the victory over sin and death.

Celebrant
As we celebrate the risen Christ,
let us pray to the God of life,
in whom we live.

Reader
That the Church of God
may be bursting with new life,
filled with the love that takes even death in its stride;
that new and mature Christians together,
all in their various ministries,
may work in God's strength
for the coming kingdom.

Silence

You are our God:
who does all things well.

That the inhabitants of our planet
may recognise God's glory all around,
co-operate in the sharing of his gifts,
and cultivate the habit of caring love.

Silence

You are our God:
who does all things well.

That God will bless our homes and families,
our places of work and leisure,
with new life and the hope of new possibilities
touching the ordinary with beauty and joy.

Silence

You are our God:
who does all things well.

That all who feel trapped or imprisoned –
physically, mentally or spiritually –
may feel the stones rolled away
and new light pouring into their lives.

Silence

You are our God:
who does all things well.

That those who have died to this earthly life
may find the fullness of God's eternity,
flooded with the light of his love.

Silence

You are our God:
who does all things well.

With Mary in her Easter joy
we make our prayer:
Hail, Mary . . .

We pray for our own intentions now,
in silence filled with joy.

Silence

Celebrant
Father, in the name of the risen Jesus,
we ask you to bring the hope,
healing and joy of the Resurrection
to all these people for whom we pray.
Amen.

SECOND SUNDAY OF EASTER

Our faith in the risen Christ
is bound to affect the way we live.

Celebrant
Knowing that the risen Christ is here among us,
let us pray in his name
for the Church and for the world.

Reader
We pray for God's blessing
on every group of Christians worshipping today
all over the world;
and we pray for all who doubt the truth.
We pray that our hearts
may be set ablaze with love,
and that we may walk as children of light.

Silence

My Lord and my God!
My Lord and my God!

We pray for all the areas of the world
which are torn apart by hatred and violence,
famine, disease, or religious differences;
we pray for an end to war
and a deeper commitment to peace.

Silence

My Lord and my God!
My Lord and my God!

We pray for those who face family rejection
if they become Christians,
and for all families divided by beliefs
or persecuted for their faith.
We pray for the children of our church
that they may grow up strong in the faith
with good role models to guide them.

Silence

My Lord and my God!
My Lord and my God!

We pray for those who wake up
to the prospect of another day filled with pain;
for those who long for someone
to spend time with them, enjoying their company;
and we pray for sight that notices needs.

Silence

My Lord and my God!
My Lord and my God!

We pray for those who mourn,
and we pray for those they love and miss,
commending all who have died
to the everlasting arms of the God of love,
in whom there is life in all its fullness.

Silence

My Lord and my God!
My Lord and my God!

We make our prayers with those of Mary,
whose trust made our salvation possible:
Hail, Mary . . .

In the silence of God's attentive love,
we name our particular petitions.

Silence

Celebrant
Trusting in your immense compassion, Father,
we offer you our prayers
and ask you to hear us,
through Jesus Christ.
Amen.

Third Sunday of Easter

Having redeemed us by his death,
Jesus can offer us the forgiveness of our sin,
which sets us free to live.

Celebrant
May God be glorified now,
as we commit ourselves to the work of prayer,
interceding for those in all kinds of need.

Reader
In our worship,
and our openness to the Spirit of life,
in the Church's longing and outreach,
in the priests, the people,
in all seekers and honest doubters,
we pray that,

in all this:
God may be glorified.

Silence

In the welfare programmes
and peace-making missions,
in the struggle to uphold justice,
in the aid given to the hungry and homeless,
we pray that,

in all this:
God may be glorified.

Silence

In the loving and costly commitment
of mothers and fathers, brothers and sisters,
daughters and sons,
in the determination to forgive and forgive,
in all the lives shared and cherished,
we pray that,

in all this:
God may be glorified.

Silence

In the work of nursing, comforting and healing,
in the daily patient struggle
with pain and weakness,
and in the practical, good-humoured caring,
we pray that,

in all this:
God may be glorified.

Silence

In the twilight years and the facing of death,
in lives well lived and now breaking into eternity,
we pray that,

in all this:
God may be glorified.

Silence

With Mary, Mother of our Redeemer,
we make our prayer:
Hail, Mary . . .

We name in silence now,
any known to us
with particular needs or burdens.

Silence

Celebrant
Heavenly Father,
slow to anger and quick to forgive,
immerse us in your Spirit
and let your will be done in our lives,
through Jesus Christ.
Amen.

Fourth Sunday of Easter

*'I am the Good Shepherd
and I lay down my life for the sheep.'*

Celebrant
The Lord is our Shepherd;
knowing his care for us, let us pray.

Reader
We pray for all who shepherd others
as bishops and pastors,
and for all in their care;
for Christians threatened and under attack;
and all whose ministry feels demanding.
For a greater affection and care, one for another, in the Church.

Silence

The Lord is our Good Shepherd:
there is nothing we shall lack.

We pray for all in positions of leadership
and influence in our world,
that they may use that power for good;
for an increase in our concern
for one another's well-being, across all barriers,
and for all who are working to build community.

Silence

The Lord is our Good Shepherd:
there is nothing we shall lack.

We pray for those who are wandering, lost and aimless,
with no idea that any Good Shepherd exists;
for those who die unaware that they are precious
and valued by the God who loved them into being.

Silence

The Lord is our Good Shepherd:
there is nothing we shall lack.

We pray for those who have died
to this earthly life,
that the Good Shepherd,
who understands what it is to die,
may bring them safely home.

Silence

The Lord is our Good Shepherd:
there is nothing we shall lack.

We pray with Mary,
Mother of the Good Shepherd:
Hail, Mary . . .

In the silence of God's accepting love,
we pray our individual petitions.

Silence

Celebrant
Loving Lord, we thank you
for this opportunity to pray,
and ask you to answer our prayers
in the way that is best for us.
In the name of Jesus we pray.
Amen.

FIFTH SUNDAY OF EASTER

To produce fruit we need to be joined on to the true vine.

Celebrant
Let us pray to the Lord God Almighty,
in whom we live and move and have our being.

Reader
We want to produce good fruit in abundance;
we pray that God may nurture us
as branches of the true vine,
train and prune us where necessary,
and that our spiritual harvest may make rich wine,
wine of the kingdom.

Silence

Your kingdom, let it come!
Your will, let it be done!

We see around our world
the tragic and expensive consequences
of branches cut off from the true vine.
We pray for a seeking after the truth
and a desire to act rightly and justly
in all areas of human society.

Silence

Your kingdom, let it come!
Your will, let it be done!

We pray for those to whom we are linked
by family, friendships or work;
especially we pray for those
separated from their loved ones or their home.

Silence

Your kingdom, let it come!
Your will, let it be done!

We long for healing and wholeness
in all who suffer
and in all dysfunctional communities;
may we be guided to understand
how we might be part of the healing.

Silence

Your kingdom, let it come!
Your will, let it be done!

We know that death cannot separate us
from God's love;
in that knowledge
we commend to God's loving keeping
those who have died and all who miss them.

Silence

Your kingdom, let it come!
Your will, let it be done!

With Mary, Mother of the true vine,
we make our prayer:
Hail, Mary . . .

Confident in God's welcoming love,
we pray in silence now
for our individual needs.

Silence

Celebrant
Merciful Father, fulfil our needs
according to your loving wisdom,
through Jesus Christ.
Amen.

SIXTH SUNDAY OF EASTER

We are to love one another as Jesus loves us.

Celebrant
Knowing God's love and affection for us,
let us pray to him now.

Reader
Wherever there is friction and conflict in the Church,
and communities are divided and weakened;
may we have a greater longing for God's healing
and a deeper commitment to his forgiving love.

Silence

Help us, Lord:
to love one another.

Wherever tangled political situations
seem impossible to solve,
wherever conflicting interests threaten peace;
wherever the ears of the powerful
remain insulated against the cries of the oppressed;
may we have ears to hear the Spirit's guidance.

Silence

Help us, Lord:
to love one another.

Wherever families are dysfunctional
or children are in danger;
wherever the daily living conditions
are damaging to health and self-respect;
may God's kingdom come.

Silence

Help us, Lord:
to love one another.

Wherever the ill and injured
need comfort and assistance;
wherever the elderly and housebound
sit each day for hours alone;
may we bring love and help.

Silence

Help us, Lord:
to love one another.

Wherever people are travelling
that last journey of death,
may they be surrounded by God's love
and welcomed into heaven,
and may those who mourn be comforted.

Silence

Help us, Lord:
to love one another.

Mary's example teaches us
the power of loving response;
with her we make our prayer:
Hail, Mary . . .

Surrounded by God's love,
we pray in silence for our own needs.

Silence

Celebrant
Heavenly Father,
so unrestrictive in your mercy,
accept our prayers and fulfil our needs,
through Jesus Christ.
Amen.

THE ASCENSION OF THE LORD

*Having bought back our freedom
with the giving of his life, Jesus enters into
the full glory to which he is entitled.*

Celebrant
Rejoicing that Jesus has ascended into the heavens,
let us pray in confidence to God our Father.

Reader
We pray in thankfulness
for those who introduced us to Jesus
and who help us along our spiritual journey.
We pray for one another in this church
and for all Christians, young and old,
throughout the world.

Silence

Let the kingdom come:
let your kingdom come.

We pray with longing
for the world to be governed
in accordance with the law of love;
that all creation may be reverenced
and treated with respect.

Silence

Let the kingdom come:
let your kingdom come.

We pray with concern
for all the homes, schools and places of work
in this community;
rejoicing in all that is of God,
and asking for healing forgiveness
wherever there is discord or bitterness.

Silence

Let the kingdom come:
let your kingdom come.

We pray with hope
for the healing and restoration to wholeness
of all who are ill or troubled,
damaged or depressed.

Silence

Let the kingdom come:
let your kingdom come.

We pray with confidence
for those who have come to the end
of their earthly lives,
that they may be given merciful judgement
and welcomed into the glory of heaven.

Silence

Let the kingdom come:
let your kingdom come.

We pray with Mary,
sharing her joy at her Son's Ascension:
Hail, Mary . . .

In silence now,
we bring to our heavenly Father
our own particular concerns.

Silence

Celebrant
God of all mercy,
our hope and our joy,
we ask you to hear our prayers,
through Christ Jesus.
Amen.

SEVENTH SUNDAY OF EASTER

Although now hidden from our sight,
Jesus lives for ever, and in him we can live
the Resurrection life even while we are on earth.

Celebrant
Let us pray together to our heavenly Father,
knowing his love for us.

Reader
As the Church,
we are called to do God's will,
to live his way
and to serve one another in love.
We pray that we may be empowered to do this.

Silence

Lord, we wait on you:
fill us, Holy Spirit of God.

We pray that our states and kingdoms
may display love, truth, justice and mercy,
that the walls of prejudice may be broken
and bridges of reconciliation and trust be built.

Silence

Lord, we wait on you:
fill us, Holy Spirit of God.

May our children be safely and lovingly nurtured,
our elderly valued,
our homes be places of welcome and warmth.

Silence

Lord, we wait on you:
fill us, Holy Spirit of God.

We pray for healing
for those whose lives are aching and weary;

for comfort and reassurance
for all who are imprisoned by fears and hate.

Silence

Lord, we wait on you:
fill us, Holy Spirit of God.

We commit our loved ones who have died
into God's safekeeping for ever.
May we all be worthy to enter eternal life.

Silence

Lord, we wait on you:
fill us, Holy Spirit of God.

We pray with Mary,
Mother of the Church:
Hail, Mary . . .

In the knowledge that God is listening,
we make our private petitions
and thanksgivings.

Silence

Celebrant
Trusting in your love for us, Father,
and full of hope in your promise to hear us,
we offer you these prayers,
in the name of Jesus Christ, your Son.
Amen.

PENTECOST

*The Holy Spirit of God is poured out in power
on the expectant disciples, just as Jesus promised.*

Celebrant
In the power of the Holy Spirit,
let us pray.

Reader
For a fresh in-breathing of life and power
in each church community,
which breaks down our barriers
and sets us on fire with God's love.

Silence

Come, Holy Spirit:
Holy Spirit, come!

For the grace to see this world
and its needs and problems
through the eyes of love, hope,
justice and mercy;
for the grace to abandon prejudice
and build bridges of reconciliation.

Silence

Come, Holy Spirit:
Holy Spirit, come!

For the Spirit of loving kindness
to fill our homes, schools and places of work;
for family rifts to be healed
and long-standing conflicts resolved.

Silence

Come, Holy Spirit:
Holy Spirit, come!

For the restoration of those who are sick
to wholeness and well-being;

for courage and patience in all suffering,
and for good to be distilled
from every painful, destructive experience.

Silence

Come, Holy Spirit:
Holy Spirit, come!

For God's merciful judgement
on those who have died,
and the opportunity for us all
to prepare carefully for meeting God
face to face.

Silence

Come, Holy Spirit:
Holy Spirit, come!

We join our prayers with those of Mary,
who joyfully received the Holy Spirit:
Hail, Mary . . .

Refreshed in the Holy Spirit,
we approach our loving Father
with our private petitions.

Silence

Celebrant
Loving Father,
rejoicing in your strength and fellowship,
we lay these prayers before you,
through Jesus Christ.
Amen.

TRINITY SUNDAY

The mysterious and holy nature of the one true God
is beyond our understanding, but it is both communal harmony
and individual personality, Father, Son and Holy Spirit.

Celebrant
Let us pray to the Father
through the Son
and in the power of the Holy Spirit.

Reader
May the Church reflect the community and unity
within the Trinity;
may there be Godly harmony, shared ministry,
mutual support and encouragement in the faith.

Silence

May your will be done:
on earth as it is in heaven.

May the world's leaders
seek not personal power but the public good;
may conflicts be faced honestly
and needs recognised and met;
may all our communities be built up
on what is good, true, just and right.

Silence

May your will be done:
on earth as it is in heaven.

May there be love and respect
for one another in every household;
may there be mutual support
and thoughtfulness, consideration and trust.

Silence

May your will be done:
on earth as it is in heaven.

May the hearts' cries for help be heard;
the tears collected and the fears quieted;
may suffering be eased and guilt erased
through your healing love.

Silence

May your will be done:
on earth as it is in heaven.

May the dead rise to new and eternal life,
freed from their aching and restored for ever.

Silence

May your will be done:
on earth as it is in heaven.

Remembering Mary's special vocation,
we make our prayer with her:
Hail, Mary . . .

In silence filled with love,
we pray our individual petitions.

Silence

Celebrant
Heavenly Father,
eternal and always present,
we offer you these prayers
in the name of Jesus.
Amen.

CORPUS CHRISTI

In bread and wine at the Last Supper,
Jesus offers himself, the Lamb of God
who takes away the sins of the world.

Celebrant
Gathered as the Body of Christ,
let us pray together to our heavenly Father.

Reader
We pray for all who celebrate
the Eucharistic mysteries,
all who administer the sacrament
of the body and blood of Christ,
and all who receive it, day by day,
week by week and year by year.
Through the loving nature of this feeding
may we all grow in holiness
and bring God's life to all we meet.

Silence

In our need, Lord:
we come to you.

We pray that all who know
their hunger and thirst for real feeding
may find the spiritual nourishment they crave,
and receive new and satisfying life
through Christ our Lord.
We pray that the world may know God's love for it.

Silence

In our need, Lord:
we come to you.

We pray for the spiritual feeding of our families,
and our parish family, through word and sacrament;
may we daily draw closer to the God who loves us,

and our lives become increasingly filled with his
life as we feed on him.

Silence

In our need, Lord:
we come to you.

We pray for those who, through frailty or illness,
receive the sacrament in their homes or in hospital;
for all who are malnourished or starving,
whether physically, emotionally or spiritually.

Silence

In our need, Lord:
we come to you.

We pray for those who have died,
that in mercy they may be brought
into the eternal joy of heaven.

Silence

In our need, Lord:
we come to you.

We make our prayers with Mary,
who brought the living bread into the world:
Hail, Mary ...

Let us be still in the presence of God
and bring to him the needs and concerns
that weigh on our hearts.

Silence

Celebrant
Heavenly Father,
you nourish us by the body and blood of Jesus,
so that we can share in the life of heaven,
both now and at the end of time.
Hear our prayers and provide for us all.
Amen.

SECOND SUNDAY OF THE YEAR

Christ calls us to follow him and walk his way through our lifetime.

Celebrant
Let us pray to the God who has called us to be here,
bringing to him the cares of our Church and our world.

Reader
We pray for deeper faith among Christians,
and a readiness to respond to God's calling.
For those being called to particular ministries
and those called to change their way of living,
we pray for courage, and the grace to obey.

Silence

Unfailing love is yours, Lord:
you are our rock of refuge.

We pray for all who feel pressurised
to conform to wrong values
in order to be accepted;
for a commitment to fight evil
and cultivate good in our world.

Silence

Unfailing love is yours, Lord:
you are our rock of refuge.

We pray for the households of this parish
and God's indwelling there;
for guidance in the everyday decisions
and the times of crisis.

Silence

Unfailing love is yours, Lord:
you are our rock of refuge.

We pray for the weak, the vulnerable,
the weary and the desolated;

for those entrenched in sin
and endangering others.

Silence

Unfailing love is yours, Lord:
you are our rock of refuge.

We pray for those who have died
in God's friendship,
and give thanks for their lives.
May they be called into the light of heaven.

Silence

Unfailing love is yours, Lord:
you are our rock of refuge.

We make our prayer with Mary,
who lovingly made herself available
to God's will:
Hail, Mary . . .

In silence filled with love,
we name our particular prayer burdens.

Silence

Celebrant
Loving Father,
we thank you for calling us,
and ask you to hear these prayers we offer,
through Christ, our Saviour.
Amen.

Third Sunday of the Year

When we are called we need to respond with obedience
so that many may be brought to repentance.

Celebrant
Through the faithfulness of others
we have heard the good news.
In thankfulness, let us pray.

Reader
We thank God for all who have worked
to spread the good news in every generation,
so that we have been able to hear it.
May we, too, be faithful in passing on
the Gospel of God's love and forgiveness.

Silence

Make us lights:
to shine in the world.

We thank God for all
who have answered the call to repentance.
We pray for all peacemakers
and those striving to establish justice,
breaking the cycle of revenge with forgiveness.

Silence

Make us lights:
to shine in the world.

We thank God for every resolved conflict,
every heartfelt apology
and all open-hearted forgiveness.
We pray for all whom we have wronged
and those who have wronged us.

Silence

Make us lights:
to shine in the world.

We thank God
for the strength and wholeness he brings us,
and pray for all who are suffering.
May they be healed and comforted,
and may our hands be ready
to carry out God's loving care.

Silence

Make us lights:
to shine in the world.

We thank God for lives well lived;
for the example of those who have died
in his friendship.
May they come to know the joy of heaven.

Silence

Make us lights:
to shine in the world.

As we open our hearts to receive Jesus,
we remember Mary's receptive love,
and make our prayer with her:
Hail, Mary . . .

In silence we pray to God our Father
for our own intentions.

Silence

Celebrant
Rejoicing that we have been called
to serve you, Father,
we offer you these prayers,
along with our lives for you to use;
through Christ our Lord.
Amen.

FOURTH SUNDAY OF THE YEAR

*Jesus displays all the signs that
mark him out to be God's chosen One.*

Celebrant
As we gather in the presence
of the almighty, all-knowing God,
let us pray.

Reader
May the whole Church honour
and glorify God's holy name
in daily lives, private prayer and public worship.

Silence

Holy God:
may your will be done.

May the whole world resound with God's truth,
activate his compassion,
and be soaked in his peace.

Silence

Holy God:
may your will be done.

May all homes and households
make plenty of room for kindness and forgiveness;
clear the clutter of discontent,
and make us more thankful.

Silence

Holy God:
may your will be done.

May all who ache with sadness or physical pain
be comforted and cherished
by God's love for them.

Silence

Holy God:
may your will be done.

May the dying be surrounded with our prayers,
and those who have passed beyond death
remain safe for ever in God's keeping.

Silence

Holy God:
may your will be done.

With Mary, Mother of the Christian family,
we make our prayer:
Hail, Mary . . .

Now, in the space of silence,
we bring to God our Father
our private petitions.

Silence

Celebrant
Most merciful Father,
we ask you to accept these prayers,
through Jesus Christ.
Amen.

FIFTH SUNDAY OF THE YEAR

The good news about God is far too good to keep to ourselves.

Celebrant
We have gathered in the presence
of the one, holy God,
from whom all things take their being.
Let us pray to him now.

Reader
Wherever the sparkle of our vision has dulled,
may the Lord set us glowing once again
at the very thought of him;
may he restore our longing to draw closer to him
until our lives reflect his shining.

Silence

Who is the King of glory?
It is the Lord our God.

Wherever important and far-reaching decisions
need to be made,
wherever wrongs need righting
and justice needs to be restored,
we pray for the holy breath
of wisdom and integrity.

Silence

Who is the King of glory?
It is the Lord our God.

Wherever ongoing family conflicts need resolving,
wherever communication has broken down,
we pray for the capacity for unconditional loving,
and appreciation of every 'other'
as another child of the Father's creating.

Silence

Who is the King of glory?
It is the Lord our God.

Wherever there is pain and suffering,
whether physical, emotional, mental or spiritual,
we pray for a fulsome and holy healing,
and ask for the courage and strength
to make ourselves available
and ready to help.

Silence

Who is the King of glory?
It is the Lord our God.

As we call to mind those who have recently died
and those who will die today,
we pray for each of them,
that in their dying
they may find the greatest healing of all,
as they come into the Father's holy presence for ever.

Silence

Who is the King of glory?
It is the Lord our God.

We join our prayers with those of Mary,
the Mother of our Saviour:
Hail, Mary . . .

Now, in silence,
we pray our individual petitions
to our heavenly Father,
who has promised to hear us.

Silence

Celebrant
Almighty Father, hear the prayers we offer,
and use our bodies, minds and spirits
in establishing your kingdom.
In the name of Jesus we pray.
Amen.

SIXTH SUNDAY OF THE YEAR

Jesus wants to heal us to wholeness,
and to him no one is untouchable.

Celebrant
Let us come to ask for the healing touch of our God
in the Church and in the world.

Reader
The God of humility, in his desire to save us,
was willing to share our human brokenness;
as the Body of Christ, may the Church share
that willingness to be vulnerable
in order to serve in love.

Silence

Good physician:
heal us.

God's power and authority is gracious and merciful;
may all those with authority in our world
be inspired to act with mercy and compassion,
so that the way may be opened
for the kingdom to be established.

Silence

Good physician:
heal us.

May we all have the strength
to drive far from our homes and communities
all rejection and devaluing,
all justification for barriers;
and may we have the courage to reach out in love.

Silence

Good physician:
heal us.

May God's compassion shock us
into seeing more clearly the ache of those
whom society rejects and overlooks;
the wounds of the discarded
and socially embarrassing.
May we reach out where others turn away.

Silence

Good physician:
heal us.

We remember those who, healed for ever,
live with God in the fullness of life.
We pray that we too may come
to share the life which has no ending.

Silence

Good physician:
heal us.

With pray with Mary,
solace and comforter:
Hail, Mary . . .

In silence filled with love,
we pray for those known to us
who need healing.

Silence

Celebrant
Father, your amazing compassion
fills us with wonder;
in joy and thankfulness we offer you
our praise and intercession
through the person of Jesus.
Amen.

Seventh Sunday of the Year

The Son of Man has authority on earth to forgive sins.

Celebrant
In the sure knowledge that God cherishes us,
let us pray to him now.

Reader
Our heavenly Father is so full of forgiveness and mercy;
may the Church be filled to the brim with such holiness
that our understanding deepens daily,
and all our work and worship glorifies his name.

Silence

Holy God:
release in us your praise.

Our heavenly Father is so wise and perceptive;
may he give us the grace to share in the healing
between factions and nations,
guided by the Spirit.

Silence

Holy God:
release in us your praise.

Our heavenly Father is so comforting and kind;
may we notice the needs around us,
in our families, friends and colleagues,
and respond to them in love.

Silence

Holy God:
release in us your praise.

We bring to our heavenly Father
our sisters and brothers whose joints are stiff
and whose bodies cannot move freely;
we give thanks for their courage and example;

and pray that God will help their spirits to dance
and fill their hearts with joy.

Silence

Holy God:
release in us your praise.

We commend those who have recently died
to the everlasting care of the Father,
and may those who mourn their going
be comforted.

Silence

Holy God:
release in us your praise.

We make our prayer with Mary,
merciful Mother of Jesus:
Hail, Mary . . .

Confident in God's restoring love,
we pray silently now
for our personal concerns.

Silence

Celebrant
Heavenly Father, so full of power
and yet so personally involved with us,
accept these prayers
and let your will be done in our lives;
through Jesus Christ we pray.
Amen.

EIGHTH SUNDAY OF THE YEAR

The long-expected bridegroom is Christ,
and the Church is his bride. We cannot half-attend the wedding feast,
but must wholeheartedly join in the celebrations.

Celebrant
Let us pray to the God of glory,
revealed to us in his Son, Jesus.

Reader
As we listen to the Father's beloved Son,
we pray that we do not fail to hear his will for us
or share his longing for the world to be saved.

Silence

Let us worship the Lord:
in the beauty of holiness.

We pray for an increase in our desire
to enter into one another's suffering and hardship,
to share the world's resources fairly
with one another,
and recognise all humanity as brothers and sisters.

Silence

Let us worship the Lord:
in the beauty of holiness.

We pray for the grace
to not take one another for granted,
but wake each morning ready to notice the Christ
in each person we see and speak to;
and reverence the Father's hidden presence
in all creation.

Silence

Let us worship the Lord:
in the beauty of holiness.

In our prayer we stand alongside
all who are too weak to pray, or too confused;
may all who are suffering
sense the Father's love and comfort,
and be given strength to persevere,
and peace of mind and spirit.

Silence

Let us worship the Lord:
in the beauty of holiness.

We commend to God's eternal presence
those who have recently died,
that they may rest in peace and rise in glory.

Silence

Let us worship the Lord:
in the beauty of holiness.

We make our prayer with Mary,
the chosen one of God:
Hail, Mary . . .

Together in silence,
we name those known to us
who need our prayers.

Silence

Celebrant
Father, we have so often experienced
your loving kindness in our lives;
accept now these prayers and answer them
in the way that is best for your creation,
through Christ our Lord.
Amen.

NINTH SUNDAY OF THE YEAR

Jesus has the words of eternal life –
he sheds light on a right attitude to the Law.

Celebrant
Through Jesus
we are shown God's compassion and mercy;
let us pray to the Father for that love in our lives,
in the Church and in the world.

Reader
Let compassion and mercy
be the hallmarks of our church life
and all its activities;
may they shine in all our behaviour,
our conversations and activities.

Silence

Lord of love:
let only your will be done.

Let compassion and mercy
take root in every institution, policy and structure;
let them challenge accepted wrongs
and disturb complacency.

Silence

Lord of love:
let only your will be done.

Let compassion and mercy
guard every doorway and fill every room;
let them colour each encounter
and drive every decision.

Silence

Lord of love:
let only your will be done.

Let compassion and mercy
transform our attitudes
to all whose illness or frailty
makes them marginalised, ignored or despised.
Let there be healing of all damaged self-perception,
and restoration of jarred human dignity.

Silence

Lord of love:
let only your will be done.

Let compassion and mercy
accompany the dying
and welcome them into eternity.

Silence

Lord of love:
let only your will be done.

We join our prayers with those of Mary,
Mother of the Lord of the Sabbath:
Hail, Mary . . .

To the Lord who brings us life,
we pour out our private petitions
and thanksgivings.

Silence

Celebrant
In praise and gratitude
we offer you these prayers, Father,
through Jesus Christ.
Amen.

TENTH SUNDAY OF THE YEAR

*Anyone who does God's will is
considered a close family member of Jesus.*

Celebrant
As members of God's family,
let us pray together to our heavenly Father.

Reader
That as family members of the Church of God
we may show his likeness by doing his will;
that those visiting our churches
may find there God's beauty and truth,
open-hearted loving and a unity of purpose.

Silence

Father:
let your will be done.

That as members of the human race
we may work together, share resources,
respect and learn from one another.
That leaders may inspire collective good,
and those with vision be valued and heard.

Silence

Father:
let your will be done.

That we may give both support and space
to those we love and nurture;
that those of our own families
who do not yet know God
may come to understand the depth
of his love for them.

Silence

Father:
let your will be done.

That all who come to Jesus in need
may find in him forgiveness, healing
and wholeness of body, mind and spirit,
strength to cope with their difficulties
and a constant inner renewing.

Silence

Father:
let your will be done.

That as those coming to death
roll up the tents of their earthly existence,
they may be welcomed into the eternal home
prepared for them by their loving God.

Silence

Father:
let your will be done.

We pray now with Mary,
whose willing obedience
made our salvation possible:
Hail, Mary . . .

In silence, now,
we approach our loving Father
with our private petitions.

Silence

Celebrant
Most merciful Father,
who knows us so well,
accept our prayers
through Christ Jesus.
Amen.

ELEVENTH SUNDAY OF THE YEAR

From small beginnings, and by God's power,
the kingdom of heaven grows.

Celebrant
Let us pray to the God of heaven and earth
for the growth of the kingdom.

Reader
May the kingdom grow
in clusters of Christians all over the world;
may it grow as hearts are warmed
by encounter with the living God;
nourished by word and sacrament,
private prayer and public worship.

Silence

Lord of heaven:
let the kingdom grow!

May the kingdom grow
in states, empires and monarchies,
in the crowded streets of cities
and in the scattered rural communities;
in all decision-making and all spending.

Silence

Lord of heaven:
let the kingdom grow!

May the kingdom grow
in every human shelter and home,
every place of work and education,
in each conversation and
in our mutual care of one another.

Silence

Lord of heaven:
let the kingdom grow!

May the kingdom grow
to bring peace and healing
wherever there is pain or sadness;
to bring reassurance, comfort, courage and hope.

Silence

Lord of heaven:
let the kingdom grow!

In the knowledge that we must all face judgement,
we pray for those who have died,
thanking God for his loving mercy,
and entrusting our loved ones
to God's safekeeping.

Silence

Lord of heaven:
let the kingdom grow!

We pray with Mary,
who nurtured our Lord in his earthly life:
Hail, Mary . . .

Knowing that God our Father is listening,
we pray in silence
for our own needs and cares.

Silence

Celebrant
Father, we lay our needs and cares before you,
and ask you to hear us,
through Christ.
Amen.

Twelfth Sunday of the Year

What kind of person is this?
Even the wind and waves obey him.

Celebrant
As residents of God's universe,
let us pray now to our loving Creator.

Reader
We pray for those in positions of authority
in the Church all over the world
and in each gathered community;
that in all the storms
we may be enabled to hear God's calming voice
and deepen our trust in him.

Silence

Lord of all truth and goodness,
calm our fears:
and teach us your peace.

We pray for those with political and military power,
and all whose decisions affect many lives.
May they speak the Spirit's truth into motives,
the Son's honour into actions,
and the Father's vision of peace into every conflict.

Silence

Lord of great power and majesty,
calm our fears:
and teach us your peace.

We pray for all single people,
couples, communal groups and families,
as they weather their storms
and learn from them;
may all who have the care of others
be given the capacity to bring peace and calm fears.

Silence

Lord of all compassion and mercy,
calm our fears:
and teach us your peace.

We pray for those
whose minds and hearts are in turmoil,
whose lives lurch from crisis to crisis;
for those who find their lives shattered
by illness or injury;
for peace in those threatening storms
and a settling of all anxiety.

Silence

Lord of all healing,
calm our fears:
and teach us your peace.

We pray for those who are dying alone,
unnoticed or unprepared;
we commend those who have died
to God's merciful forgiveness
and eternal tranquillity.

Silence

Lord of eternity,
calm our fears:
and teach us your peace.

We pray with Mary,
who served God fearlessly:
Hail, Mary . . .

Trusting in God our Father,
we name our particular prayer burdens.

Silence

Celebrant
Father, rejoicing that you are in overall charge
of all creation,
we offer these prayers,
through Christ Jesus.
Amen.

THIRTEENTH SUNDAY OF THE YEAR

God's power can reach even into death and draw out life.

Celebrant
As God has called us by name
out into full, abundant life,
let us lay before him now our concerns
for the Church and for the world.

Reader
May all the built-up layers
of complacency or despondency,
of over-comfortable familiarity
or under-active expectation
be removed from the Church
and from our lives,
until we see again
with the freshness and wonder of deepened faith.

Silence

Lord, we believe:
help our unbelief.

We call to mind societies and systems of our world.
May our assumptions be questioned
and our destructive choices challenged;
may the unnoticed scales of prejudice which blind us
be broken away,
so that our world may increasingly come
under the reign of justice, righteousness and love.

Silence

Lord, we believe:
help our unbelief.

May our pride be replaced with humility
until we learn from young children
the lessons of wonder and trust.
May the childlike be kept as a living flame
in all of us, whatever our age,

and enable us to rediscover God's glory
all around us.

Silence

Lord, we believe:
help our unbelief.

As the sick were brought to Jesus
by their loved ones,
so now in prayer we bring all those
whom we long to be healed.
May they hear the Lord's voice
and sense his touch.

Silence

Lord, we believe:
help our unbelief.

Earth-bound, we grieve
at the loss of loved ones through death;
yet we also rejoice
that they have been called by the Lord
into the fullness of everlasting life.

Silence

Lord, we believe:
help our unbelief.

With Mary who gave us her Son,
we make our prayer:
Hail, Mary . . .

In the silence of God's generous love,
we name those known to us
who need our prayers.

Silence

Celebrant
Father, we thank you
for drawing us here to pray,
and ask you to hear us,
through Jesus Christ.
Amen.

Fourteenth Sunday of the Year

If we are not ready to listen to the truth, we will not hear it.

Celebrant
God has drawn us down many different routes
to this shared worship today.
Let us still our bodies
and alert our minds and hearts in his presence.

Reader
We are the Body of Christ
because the Spirit binds us together.
We pray for a real concern and love for one another,
supportive and encouraging,
without malice or bickering,
so that we can be sent out
strong in our weakness and littleness.

Silence

Heavenly Father, give us your grace:
to hear your word with joy.

All the kingdoms and states
are answerable to divine authority,
and much evil is allowed to flourish
through the silence of good people;
we pray for the courage to speak out the truth,
whether it is popular or not.

Silence

Heavenly Father, give us your grace:
to hear your word with joy.

May all our listening
at home, on the phone, at school and at work
be done with our full attention to God's voice
and to one another,
happy to grow wiser through each conversation.

Silence

Heavenly Father, give us your grace:
to hear your word with joy.

We pray for those
whose pain screams silently and incessantly;
for those who have no one to confide in,
no one to listen.
May the love of the Lord enfold them,
his peace calm them
and his healing transform them.

Silence

Heavenly Father, give us your grace:
to hear your word with joy.

In all our life and in all our living
may we be prepared for the life to come;
we commend to the Lord's keeping all those
who have recently made their journey through death.

Silence

Heavenly Father, give us your grace:
to hear your word with joy.

Mary showed us how to listen;
we join our prayers with hers:
Hail, Mary . . .

We bring our personal petitions now
to God our Father, who hears us.

Silence

Celebrant
Father, we ask you to fulfil our prayers
to your glory;
in Jesus' name we pray.
Amen.

FIFTEENTH SUNDAY OF THE YEAR

*Those who speak out God's will are bound
to be vulnerable to rejection and abuse.*

Celebrant
In humility and love
let us draw near to our God
and pray to him now.

Reader
We pray that our lives
may be upright and holy;
that our church communities may shine
with goodness and love, humility and truth;
we pray for all leaning lives to be straightened up
through your merciful forgiveness.

Silence

Holy God, scatter all darkness:
and bathe our world in your light.

We pray that many may be empowered
to recognise evil and fight against it;
to discern warning signs and speak them out;
to notice the sparks of love and goodness
and celebrate them.

Silence

Holy God, scatter all darkness:
and bathe our world in your light.

We pray that our households
and neighbourhoods,
our places of work and leisure,
may be arenas of praise and thankfulness,
not only in the comfort zones
but particularly through the disturbed
and difficult times.

Silence

Holy God, scatter all darkness:
and bathe our world in your light.

We pray for those in prison;
for those leading cruel and violent lives;
for all victims of oppression or abuse;
for all who suffer mental anguish or physical pain.

Silence

Holy God, scatter all darkness:
and bathe our world in your light.

We pray for those who have died,
that they, and we in our turn, may be given
merciful judgement through Jesus our Saviour,
and brought into the unquenchable light of heaven.

Silence

Holy God, scatter all darkness:
and bathe our world in your light.

We pray with Mary,
who mothered the Son of God:
Hail, Mary . . .

In silence now,
we bring to God's love
the special needs and concerns
known to us individually.

Silence

Celebrant
With great joy, Father,
in the knowledge
that we can trust you unconditionally,
we offer you our prayers,
through Jesus Christ.
Amen.

SIXTEENTH SUNDAY OF THE YEAR

*Like a good shepherd, Jesus sees the needs
of his people and always responds with love.*

Celebrant
Knowing God's love and concern for us all,
let us settle ourselves in his presence
and pray to him now.

Reader
Recognising the brokenness and disunity
of Christ's Church,
we pray that he may draw us closer to one another
as we draw closer to him;
we pray for all our Christian brothers and sisters
in this neighbourhood,
and for all who are searching
for meaning in their lives.

Silence

The Lord is my shepherd:
there is nothing I shall want.

With the noise of global conflicts
and human deprivation
thundering in our ears,
with the questions and doubts clamouring,
we pray that the Lord may shepherd our humanness
and lead us in the secret places of the heart.

Silence

The Lord is my shepherd:
there is nothing I shall want.

With the statistics of family life
challenging our values,
and with the pressures to conform to norms
in conflict with God's will,
we pray for a sound and centred wisdom
in all our daily living and life choices.

Silence

The Lord is my shepherd:
there is nothing I shall want.

With the stressed and overburdened,
the overworked and the unemployed,
we pray for balanced lives;
for physical, mental and spiritual health;
for patience in times of trouble,
and direction in times of confusion.

Silence

The Lord is my shepherd:
there is nothing I shall want.

As we remember with love and gratitude
the lives of those who have died in faith,
we commend them to eternal rest in the Lord
and his unchanging affection.

Silence

The Lord is my shepherd:
there is nothing I shall want.

We pray with Mary,
whose Son became our Good Shepherd:
Hail, Mary . . .

God our Father loves us;
in this silence
we name our particular petitions.

Silence

Celebrant
Father, in the sure knowledge
of your promise to answer the prayers
of all who are faithful,
we offer you our cares and concerns,
through Jesus Christ.
Amen.

Seventeenth Sunday of the Year

*Out of God's riches, a great crowd is fed
and satisfied from a small offering of food.*

Celebrant
Knowing that our loving God
supplies all our needs,
let us pray to him now
on behalf of the Church and the world.

Reader
We pray for the Church
with all its varied ministries;
for the youngest to the oldest baptised members;
for those of mellow faith
and those who struggle with doubts.

Silence

Loving Father:
give us today our daily bread.

We pray for the strength
of a new commitment within ourselves
to pray the news each day
and share the pain we read about,
longing for peace and justice
in a world tense with aggression
and distorted with selfishness.

Silence

Loving Father:
give us today our daily bread.

We pray that the Lord may work in,
and transform, our homes and our relationships.
In all our meetings and conflicts
and all differences of opinion
may we work to the glory of God.

Silence

Loving Father:
give us today our daily bread.

We pray for all who suffer
or are heavily burdened;
we pray for their comfort and refreshment,
wholeness and restoration,
but above all for the consciousness
of Christ's presence in their pain,
and his love for them.

Silence

Loving Father:
give us today our daily bread.

We pray for the faithful souls
entering by the gate of physical death
that they may have eternal life.

Silence

Loving Father:
give us today our daily bread.

We make our prayer with Mary,
who fed and clothed her precious Son:
Hail, Mary . . .

As God our Father listens with love,
we name those we know
who are in any particular need.

Silence

Celebrant
Father, your generosity draws us
to love more deeply;
hear us as we pray,
and use us in fulfilling our prayers.
We pray through Jesus Christ.
Amen.

216

EIGHTEENTH SUNDAY OF THE YEAR

*Jesus is the Bread of Life who satisfies our hunger
and sustains us on our journey to heaven.*

Celebrant
Let us pray to the God who loves us,
knows our needs, and provides for us.

Reader
As the travelling people of God,
we pray for a deepening hunger
for the things of God
and a loosening of our grip
on all the wants and expectations
which prevent us from moving forward God's way.

Silence

Feed us, Father:
with the Bread of Life.

As brothers and sisters with the whole of creation,
we pray for respect and reverence among people
regardless of wealth or status;
for responsible sharing of resources
and consideration for the natural world
of our fragile and beautiful planet.

Silence

Feed us, Father:
with the Bread of Life.

As we prepare and eat our food each day,
we pray for those who grow and manufacture it,
distribute and sell it, shop for it and cook it,
and for those with whom we share food.
May we all be built up with the spiritual feeding
which sustains us for ever.

Silence

Feed us, Father:
with the Bread of Life.

As we ask for daily bread,
we pray for those who are physically starving,
for all who hunger emotionally
or try to survive on spiritual junk food;
for those who mistrust God's feeding.

Silence

Feed us, Father:
with the Bread of Life.

As we remember with love
those who have journeyed through physical death,
we pray that, nourished by the Bread of Life,
they may travel on eagles' wings
into the brightness of eternal life.

Silence

Feed us, Father:
with the Bread of Life.

We pray now with Mary,
who so tenderly nurtured her holy child:
Hail, Mary . . .

Meeting our heavenly Father
in the stillness of silence,
let us bring to him
our own particular cares and concerns.

Silence

Celebrant
Father, we can never thank you enough
for what you have done for us,
and for the way you are transforming our lives;
with grateful hearts we offer you these prayers,
through Jesus Christ.
Amen.

Nineteenth Sunday of the Year

Just as bread is the visible form of life-giving nourishment,
so Jesus is the visible form of God's life-giving love.

Celebrant
Let us pray to our God
as we worship him in Spirit and in truth.

Reader
We pray for all who are commissioned and called
to work as leaders and prophets in the Church.
We pray for greater discernment
of the Lord's presence
and his will in our Christian communities,
and a clearing away of all that obscures our vision.

Silence

Heavenly Father, open our eyes:
to see your glory.

We pray against the cynicism
and complacency that deaden wonder.
In the ordinary things of life
may we detect love and wisdom;
through the everyday events
may we encounter Christ, walking alongside us.

Silence

Heavenly Father, open our eyes:
to see your glory.

We pray for breadwinners
and sandwich makers, and all food growers;
for the Spirit's presence in kitchens, dining rooms,
canteens, restaurants and bars;
wherever people gather to eat together.

Silence

Heavenly Father, open our eyes:
to see your glory.

We pray for those whose emotional damage
makes trusting and receiving
seem threatening and dangerous.
We pray for peace of mind for the anxious,
and hope for all who are close to despair.

Silence

Heavenly Father, open our eyes:
to see your glory.

We pray for those
who have reached the boundary of death,
that in faith they may journey through it
and out into the unconfined space
and joy of heaven.

Silence

Heavenly Father, open our eyes:
to see your glory.

We pray with Mary,
our spiritual Mother:
Hail, Mary . . .

Upheld by God's grace,
we pray now in silence
for any who specially need our prayer.

Silence

Celebrant
Father, we acknowledge
our total dependence on you,
and ask you to hear us as we pray,
through Jesus Christ.
Amen.

TWENTIETH SUNDAY OF THE YEAR

God's wisdom may appear foolishness
without the God-given grace to understand.

Celebrant
As we gather, conscious of our need of wisdom,
let us pray to our wise and loving God.

Reader
In all the decision-making,
problems and challenges of our church,
we ask for wise counsel and encouragement;
in all our worship and outreach.

Silence

Wise and loving God:
quieten us to hear your voice.

In all the clashes of needs and wants,
the half-forgotten hurts that drive aggression,
the half-remembered grievances,
barbed with revenge,
in all the world's raging and protesting,
we pray for the spirit of peace and reconciliation.

Silence

Wise and loving God:
quieten us to hear your voice.

In the daily batch of misunderstandings,
conflicting loyalties, negotiations and compromise,
may the Spirit walk among us
in our homes and places of work,
whispering sanity and mutual respect.

Silence

Wise and loving God:
quieten us to hear your voice.

For those engulfed by pain
or enslaved by addiction,
we pray for hope and healing;
may the Lord bless all those
whose minds think simply
and rely on others for basic care.

Silence

Wise and loving God:
quieten us to hear your voice.

May all who have left this life
in the Father's friendship
be gathered into his keeping for ever;
we pray too for those approaching death,
that they may know his love
surrounding them across time and eternity.

Silence

Wise and loving God:
quieten us to hear your voice.

We join our prayers with those of Mary,
whose spirit was always peaceful:
Hail, Mary . . .

Together in silence now,
we make our private petitions.

Silence

Celebrant
Most loving and merciful Father,
we ask you to take over our lives
and live through them,
and accept these our prayers
in the name of Jesus.
Amen.

TWENTY-FIRST SUNDAY OF THE YEAR

'To whom else could we go?
You alone have the words of eternal life.'

Celebrant
We have chosen to serve the Lord.
Let us pray to him now.

Reader
We pray for those whose faith
is being challenged or undermined
by inner doubts or outside influences.
We pray for those who build up our faith
and all who strive to proclaim the Gospel
in language that people understand.

Silence

Holy God, we believe:
help our unbelief.

We pray for our torn and fragmented world,
wrestling to equate the deep yearning for peace
with the instinctive urge
for gratification and power;
that many may have the courage
to walk God's way.

Silence

Holy God, we believe:
help our unbelief.

We pray for our loved ones;
for those who lift our hearts
and those who turn our hair grey.
We pray for those we instinctively warm to
and those with whom
there are frequent misunderstandings.

Silence

Holy God, we believe:
help our unbelief.

We pray for all who are marginalised,
scorned or rejected;
for those isolated through illness or imprisonment;
for those who feel that no one understands.
May the Lord surround them all with such love
that they may know they are precious.

Silence

Holy God, we believe:
help our unbelief.

We pray for those approaching death,
that through our prayers
they may know themselves
accompanied with love on that journey.
We pray for those who have died,
that they may come to know the full joy of heaven.

Silence

Holy God, we believe:
help our unbelief.

Now we join our prayers with those of Mary,
the Mother of Jesus:
Hail, Mary . . .

In silence, we name any we know
who especially need our prayer.

Silence

Celebrant
In great thankfulness
for all your blessings to us,
heavenly Father,
we offer you these prayers,
through Jesus Christ.
Amen.

TWENTY-SECOND SUNDAY OF THE YEAR

*We need to be careful never to replace
the timeless commands of God with man-made traditions.*

Celebrant
Our God is the source of all holiness;
with the needs of the Church and the world
close to our hearts,
let us pray to the only one
who can renew and redeem.

Reader
Aware of our temptation
to place our trust in rules and traditions,
we pray for a release in the Church
of such a desire to serve the living God
that nothing is allowed to get in the way of that.

Silence

Into your hands, O Lord:
we commit the future.

We recognise in ourselves
the universal dangerous wants and cravings
which are cultivated because they make money.
May we have such a loathing of evil
that there will be international co-operation
and individual responsibility in fighting it
and building one another up in love.

Silence

Into your hands, O Lord:
we commit the future.

May our homes, schools and churches
reflect and engender the Godly values
of mutual care, respect and responsibility,
of integrity and forgiveness.

Silence

Into your hands, O Lord:
we commit the future.

We stand alongside all who are hurting
in body, mind or spirit;
all who need courage, support or practical help.
May we be willing to become
part of God's answer
to our prayers for them.

Silence

Into your hands, O Lord:
we commit the future.

We commit to the Father's keeping
those who have died to this life;
that, freed from all pain, and forgiven,
they may live in the peace and joy of heaven.

Silence

Into your hands, O Lord:
we commit the future.

Encouraged by Mary's example of obedience,
we make our prayer with her:
Hail, Mary . . .

As God's stillness fills our hearts,
we pray for our own particular needs and concerns.

Silence

Celebrant
Heavenly Father,
in your love and mercy hear our prayers,
through the mediation of Jesus Christ.
Amen.

TWENTY-THIRD SUNDAY OF THE YEAR

Jesus comes fulfilling the hope of healing to wholeness;
he shows that mercy has triumphed over judgement.

Celebrant
Let us pray to our loving and merciful God.

Reader
In gratitude for the richness and diversity
of each unique identity,
we pray for the separate members
of this Body of Christ, and our corporate nature,
that we may be filled at every level
with the living breath of God.

Silence

Father of mercy:
let your kingdom come.

In gratitude for the beauty and variety
of our landscapes and cultures, all over the world;
for starscapes and the wideness of space,
we pray that we may cherish and respect
this universe we inhabit,
and respect all those who look or sound
different from ourselves.

Silence

Father of mercy:
let your kingdom come.

In gratitude for the hope
each newborn child brings;
for the gentle gifts of laughter and friendship,
thoughtfulness and sympathy,
we pray that our eyes may see all others
with God's affection.

Silence

Father of mercy:
let your kingdom come.

In gratitude for the patient endurance
of so many who suffer so much,
we pray that they may come to know
Christ's wholeness and refreshing,
his upholding and healing.

Silence

Father of mercy:
let your kingdom come.

In gratitude for the promise of mercy
triumphing over judgement,
we commend to God's love for ever
our own loved ones who have died.

Silence

Father of mercy:
let your kingdom come.

We join our prayers with those of Mary,
who was full of compassion for others:
Hail, Mary . . .

In this silence,
we bring our particular petitions
to God our Father.

Silence

Celebrant
Father, your character is so rich in mercy;
please hear our prayers
which we offer in the name of Jesus.
Amen.

TWENTY-FOURTH SUNDAY OF THE YEAR

Loving obedience to God is shown by Jesus
to be a quality rich in courage and wisdom,
a quality to be highly respected.

Celebrant
As sons and daughters of our heavenly Father,
responding to his call,
let us bring to him our needs and concerns.

Reader
That we may all learn to think God's way
and desire to do his will above everything else;
that we may be ready to suffer if necessary,
and put ourselves out, and do that cheerfully,
considering it a privilege.

Silence

Lord, in the spirit of obedience:
we ask your guidance.

That the craving to be most powerful
may be transformed into a yearning
for mutual respect and harmony;
that wealth may not shout louder than right,
and the whisper of truth may be heard
above the clamour of expediency.

Silence

Lord, in the spirit of obedience:
we ask your guidance.

That within our homes and places of work
we may practise self-discipline in all that we say,
and in the way it is said,
using our mouths to speak wisely and positively
with love in both hearts and voices.

Silence

Lord, in the spirit of obedience:
we ask your guidance.

That those whose bodies or spirits
are heavy with suffering
may be given courage and hope,
ease from the pain, and healing to wholeness.
That we may know how best to help them.

Silence

Lord, in the spirit of obedience:
we ask your guidance.

That those who have died in faith
may rise to eternal life,
and that we may so live on earth
that we are all prepared
for meeting the Father face to face in heaven.

Silence

Lord, in the spirit of obedience:
we ask your guidance.

We make our prayer with Mary,
Mother of Jesus, the Christ:
Hail, Mary . . .

In the knowledge
that God our Father hears us,
let us name our own particular petitions.

Silence

Celebrant
Father of mercy, hear our prayers
which we offer through Jesus, the Christ.
Amen.

TWENTY-FIFTH
SUNDAY OF THE YEAR

*The truly great in God's eyes are those
who are prepared to be last of all and servant of all.*

Celebrant
Let us pray to the God of glory
in whom we live and move and have our being.

Reader
We pray that the Church may hold true
to the teaching of Jesus,
free from the worldly values of status and ambition.
We pray for a spirit of humility
to deflate all pomposity and arrogance.

Silence

Yours, Lord, is the kingdom:
yours the power and yours the glory.

We pray that all in positions of power,
authority and influence in our world
may recognise their calling to servanthood
and never lose their identity
with the needs and longings of those they serve.

Silence

Yours, Lord, is the kingdom:
yours the power and yours the glory.

We pray that all communities
may look after one another,
supporting the vulnerable, encouraging the timid,
providing practical help for all who need it,
and nurturing the young in a climate of trust.

Silence

Yours, Lord, is the kingdom:
yours the power and yours the glory.

We pray that none may be considered expendable,
or beyond our cherishing;
we pray for all who have lost heart,
through pain, suffering or sin,
that God's redeeming power may work its wonders
in the very darkest situations.

Silence

Yours, Lord, is the kingdom:
yours the power and yours the glory.

We pray that all who have wearily
struggled to death
may know the joy of burdens laid down,
and new, lasting life transforming them
through the eternal love of God.

Silence

Yours, Lord, is the kingdom:
yours the power and yours the glory.

We make our prayer with Mary,
who shared her Son's sorrows:
Hail, Mary . . .

Trustingly, we pray in silence
to our loving Lord,
who considers each one of us special.

Silence

Celebrant
Father, you always give us far more
than we can ever deserve;
please fulfil our prayers
in the way that is best for us.
We ask in the name of Jesus Christ.
Amen.

TWENTY-SIXTH SUNDAY OF THE YEAR

*Don't let your body lead you into sin and risk
exchanging eternal life for eternal punishment.*

Celebrant
Conscious of our need for God's power
in our lives, our Church and our world,
let us pray to him now.

Reader
We pray for the courage
to reject sin and evil in our own lives.
May our churches be powerhouses of the Spirit,
training and upholding us
as we live the Father's life and love in the world.

Silence

Your Law, O Lord, is perfect:
it revives the soul.

We pray for a greater awareness
of what damages souls and encourages evil,
and for widespread commitment
to addressing the dangers.
We pray for all who earn their living
through selling what destroys lives.

Silence

Your Law, O Lord, is perfect:
it revives the soul.

We pray for the young,
and the vulnerable in every community,
for all in positions of trust,
for child-minders, playgroups and schools,
for loving nurture and protection from all evil.

Silence

Your Law, O Lord, is perfect:
it revives the soul.

We pray for all long-term carers
and those they look after,
for all who are having
to learn dependence gracefully,
and those who are imprisoned by their guilt.
May the Lord work his healing love in them all,
reassuring them of his presence.

Silence

Your Law, O Lord, is perfect:
it revives the soul.

We pray that no one may be lost eternally,
that all may turn from their sin
and trust in God's mercy;
that physical death may be but the gate to heaven.
We commend to God's loving mercy
those who have recently died.

Silence

Your Law, O Lord, is perfect:
it revives the soul.

Encouraged by Mary's steadfast example,
we make our prayer with her:
Hail, Mary . . .

In silence filled with love,
we name our particular prayer burdens.

Silence

Celebrant
With thankfulness and praise
for all your blessings to us, Father,
we offer you these prayers,
through Jesus Christ.
Amen.

TWENTY-SEVENTH SUNDAY OF THE YEAR

*Human beings are made responsible
for the care of creation but are subject
to God in all aspects of their lives.*

Celebrant
Let us come before God our Maker,
making our prayers to him,
through Jesus and in the power of the Holy Spirit.

Reader
We pray that the Church may be alive
to God's beckoning,
quick to obey his will
and always ready to act in his loving service
for the good of the world.

Silence

Lord of heaven:
let your will be done.

We pray that all leaders and heads of state
may take wise advice and act responsibly
for the well-being of all.
We pray for God's guidance
in the way we manage and care for this planet,
its resources, riches and inhabitants.

Silence

Lord of heaven:
let your will be done.

We pray for all marriages,
for those seeking marriage partners
and those whose marriages are under strain.
We pray for all in close relationships,
that there may be mutual love and respect.

Silence

Lord of heaven:
let your will be done.

We pray for all who are suffering
through illness, accident or deliberate cruelty;
for refugees and all who are abused;
that through the caring of human hands
they may experience the caring hands of God.

Silence

Lord of heaven:
let your will be done.

We pray for all who have died violently
or suddenly, or with no one to miss them.
May all who have died in faith
be judged with mercy
and welcomed into eternal life.

Silence

Lord of heaven:
let your will be done.

We pray with Mary,
the Mother of the Lord:
Hail, Mary . . .

Knowing that God our Father
hears the cries of his children,
we pray in silence
for our needs and cares.

Silence

Celebrant
Father of compassion and mercy,
accept our prayers,
through the person of Jesus Christ.
Amen.

TWENTY-EIGHTH
SUNDAY OF THE YEAR

The most valuable possession is not
the wealth that owns us, but is Christ,
the Wisdom of God, who gives us untold riches.

Celebrant
Let us lay down our own agendas
and seek the face of God,
and his will for the Church and for the world.

Reader
We pray for all who are seeking God,
and for the nurturing process in this parish.
We pray for opportunities to share God's love
and draw others to meet him.

Silence

Father, your will be done:
on earth as in heaven.

We pray for all who are fighting against evil
for goodness, truth and justice,
both those who make the world news
and those whose battles are known only to God.
We pray for our country and its leaders,
that this nation may seek God.

Silence

Father, your will be done:
on earth as in heaven.

We pray that wealth and comfort may not divert us
from searching out the heart of God;
that we may hear God's challenging
and gladly respond to him;
that our homes and communities
may sparkle with God's glory.

Silence

Father, your will be done:
on earth as in heaven.

We pray for the disillusioned and depressed
and all who have lost their way in life;
we pray for those corrupted by evil,
trained in hatred and twisted by bitterness.
We pray for the transforming of these lives.

Silence

Father, your will be done:
on earth as in heaven.

We pray for those whose earthly life
has come to an end,
and for those who mourn their going.
May the dead rest in the peace and joy of heaven.

Silence

Father, your will be done:
on earth as in heaven.

We join our prayer with Mary,
who laid up treasure in heaven:
Hail, Mary . . .

As our loving Father listens in love,
we share with him our personal burdens,
joys and sorrows.

Silence

Celebrant
Father, in your great mercy,
hear these prayers we offer,
through Jesus Christ.
Amen.

TWENTY-NINTH
SUNDAY OF THE YEAR

*Even the Son of Man himself came not to be served
but to serve, and to give his life as a ransom for many.*

Celebrant
In humility and love, let us pray together
to the God of our making and redeeming.

Reader
That all Christians may fulfil their vocation
to be servants, caring for the needs of others,
obedient to their Lord in all things
and supportive of one another
in worship, prayer and deepening faith.

Silence

Into your hands, O Lord:
we commit our prayers.

That those who govern and advise
may seek out God's will
and the good of all
in each crisis, dilemma and debate.

Silence

Into your hands, O Lord:
we commit our prayers.

That we may develop the habit
of rejoicing in the opportunities to serve,
and to put ourselves out for others,
laying down our craving for praise
and importance.

Silence

Into your hands, O Lord:
we commit our prayers.

That those who suffer in mind, body and spirit
may sense the Christ close beside them,
knowing his healing and resting in his love.

Silence

Into your hands, O Lord:
we commit our prayers.

That those who have died in faith
may be welcomed into the light of heaven,
and that all who are walking in sin today
may turn away from evil, and live.

Silence

Into your hands, O Lord:
we commit our prayers.

We pray with Mary,
who knew the reality of suffering:
Hail, Mary . . .

God our Father loves us;
in silence now,
we bring our personal petitions to him.

Silence

Celebrant
Father, in your unfailing mercy,
we ask you to accept these prayers,
through Jesus Christ.
Amen.

THIRTIETH SUNDAY OF THE YEAR

*In Jesus, God gathers his scattered people
and opens their eyes to see.*

Celebrant
As children of our heavenly Father,
trusting in his will and capacity to care for us all,
let us pray.

Reader
We pray for all pastoral care in the Church,
for the ministries of listening and counselling;
the sharing of grief; the freeing from guilt.
We pray for the grace to accompany
others to Christ's healing love.

Silence

What do you want God to do for you?
Lord, we want to see.

We pray for the healing of the nations;
for a recognition of our need of God
and a turning away from all that is evil.
We pray for all in authority and worldly power,
that they may be guided along right paths.

Silence

What do you want God to do for you?
Lord, we want to see.

We pray for an increase in love for one another,
that we may be better at recognising needs
and responding to them;
that we may give more time to those we love.

Silence

What do you want God to do for you?
Lord, we want to see.

We pray for those who are blind
or partially sighted,
and those who are spiritually or emotionally blind.
We pray for the opening of eyes to see God's way
and faith to trust him through good and ill.

Silence

What do you want God to do for you?
Lord, we want to see.

We pray for those whose eyes
have shut to this world,
that they may open to the brightness
and joy of heaven.

Silence

What do you want God to do for you?
Lord, we want to see.

We pray with Mary,
whose spiritual vision was clear:
Hail, Mary . . .

To God, our heavenly Father,
we pray for our own intentions.

Silence

Celebrant
Father,
you pour out your blessings so richly on us;
with thankful hearts we praise you,
and ask you to hear our prayers,
through Jesus Christ.
Amen.

THIRTY-FIRST
SUNDAY OF THE YEAR

To love the living God with heart, soul and strength,
and to love our neighbour as ourselves
means far more than any sacrificial offerings.

Celebrant
As God's people, gathered in his presence,
let us pray.

Reader
For all who preach and teach the Gospel
in word and sacrament
throughout the worldwide Church.
For those who lead prayer groups
and Bible studies,
and all who gossip their faith to others.

Silence

O Lord our God:
in you we trust.

For all who are tortured or persecuted
for what they believe;
for the voiceless and powerless,
for the powerful and coercive.

Silence

O Lord our God:
in you we trust.

For greater respect for one another
as children of God's making;
for God's presence in each conversation,
discussion and debate,
each concern and celebration.

Silence

O Lord our God:
in you we trust.

For healing and wholeness,
mending and comforting,
calming and refreshing,
wherever lives and bodies ache.

Silence

O Lord our God:
in you we trust.

For everlasting peace in the arms of God
for those who have come to the end
of their life on earth
and comfort for all who grieve.

Silence

O Lord our God:
in you we trust.

Mary faithfully loved God and her neighbour;
let us join our prayers with hers:
Hail, Mary . . .

In the silence of our hearts,
we pray for any needs known to us personally.

Silence

Celebrant
Father, with grateful hearts for the gift of life,
we offer you these prayers,
together with ourselves
for your service;
in Jesus' name we pray.
Amen.

THIRTY-SECOND SUNDAY OF THE YEAR

Loving generosity is the hallmark of Godly giving.

Celebrant
Let us pray to our loving and generous God.

Reader
We pray that God will transform our giving
and provide us with the courage
to renounce all meanness of spirit,
until we are glad to give freely and lovingly.

Silence

Give us today our daily bread:
give us – and forgive us.

We pray that we may be good stewards
of this planet we are given to inhabit;
that all may learn to share what we have here
and look after it well for those who come after us.

Silence

Give us today our daily bread:
give us – and forgive us.

We pray that we may be more generous
in the attention we give to one another;
in allowing others to be themselves,
different from us but just as valid.

Silence

Give us today our daily bread:
give us – and forgive us.

We pray for the poor and for the rich,
for all whose lives are somehow impoverished.
We pray for those in debt
and all who are finding finances a great worry.

Silence

Give us today our daily bread:
give us – and forgive us.

We pray for those who have died,
that in God's mercy they may be welcomed
into the peace and joy of heaven.

Silence

Give us today our daily bread:
give us – and forgive us.

We join our prayers with those of Mary,
who gave of herself without stinting:
Hail, Mary . . .

In quietness now,
we pray for our own particular needs
and concerns.

Silence

Celebrant
Father, we thank you for bringing us here today,
and ask you to accept our prayers
through Jesus Christ.
Amen.

Thirty-Third
Sunday of the Year

*We are to be on our guard; great anguish will
accompany the last days, but all that is good and loving,
wise and true will be saved and celebrated for ever.*

Celebrant
As God's love has drawn us, let us pray.

Reader
That the Church may grow and flourish,
protected from evil within and without;
that in worship and ministry
God's love may be brought into places of darkness
and offer many the light of hope.

Silence

Lord our God:
show us the path of life.

That our shrinking world
may bring about co-operation
and a fresh appreciation of one another's cultures;
that we may encourage one another
in goodness, peace and love.

Silence

Lord our God:
show us the path of life.

That we may take time
to cherish our loved ones in the present moment,
and value the blessings we receive each day.

Silence

Lord our God:
show us the path of life.

That God's healing touch
may bring wholeness and peace
to those who suffer,
and hope to those who are close to despair.

Silence

Lord our God:
show us the path of life.

That God's love may surround those
travelling through death
and bring them safely to heaven.

Silence

Lord our God:
show us the path of life.

We pray now with Mary,
who showed us how to wait
with a quiet heart:
Hail, Mary . . .

As God's stillness fills our hearts,
we make our private petitions.

Silence

Celebrant
Trusting in your promise to hear us, Father,
we offer you these prayers,
through Jesus Christ.
Amen.

CHRIST THE KING

Jesus Christ is the everlasting King
whose kingdom is not of this world, but grows
in the hearts of his people and lasts for ever.

Celebrant
As children of the kingdom,
let us make our prayers to the eternal God,
who loves us.

Reader
We pray that the kingdom may come
in the worldwide communities
of those who believe in Jesus Christ –
may our lives enthrone him.

Silence

Spirit of the living God:
may your kingdom come.

We pray that the kingdom may come
in the nations of our world
and in their leadership;
for God's values to take root and grow;
for each person to be respected
as a beloved child of God.

Silence

Spirit of the living God:
may your kingdom come.

We pray that the kingdom may come
in our homes and families,
our neighbourhoods and places of work,
in all thinking, all speaking and all action.

Silence

Spirit of the living God:
may your kingdom come.

We pray that the kingdom may come
in all hospitals and surgeries,
and in every place of pain and sadness.

Silence

Spirit of the living God:
may your kingdom come.

We pray that the kingdom may come
in the final stages of earthly life,
in the journey through death,
and in the awakening to eternal life.

Silence

Spirit of the living God:
may your kingdom come.

We make our prayer with Mary,
Mother of Christ the King:
Hail, Mary . . .

The God of Peace is listening;
in this silence,
we name those we know
who are in any particular need.

Silence

Celebrant
Most merciful and loving Father,
we ask you to hear and answer our prayers
which we offer in the name of Jesus.
Amen.

YEAR C

First Sunday of Advent

The gathered hopes of generations remind us to get ourselves ready,
so that Christ's return will be a day of excitement and great joy.

Celebrant
As we think about the fulfilment of all things today,
let us speak with the God of our making.

Reader
We pray that we will all be ready
to meet God face to face,
whenever that will be.

Silence

Lord, show us how to live:
and give us the courage to go forward.

We pray that all who lead and advise
may be led and advised by the Spirit,
so that our decisions are in line
with the Father's compassionate will.

Silence

Lord, show us how to live:
and give us the courage to go forward.

We pray that our families and neighbours
may be brought into contact
with the one true, living God
and know his affection for them.

Silence

Lord, show us how to live:
and give us the courage to go forward.

We ask that, through our prayers and our actions,
those hurt by injustice may know support,
the frail, encouragement,
and the timid, reassurance.

Silence

Lord, show us how to live:
and give us the courage to go forward.

We pray that those moving into eternity
through the gate of death
may be welcomed,
and their grieving loved ones comforted.

Silence

Lord, show us how to live:
and give us the courage to go forward.

As we prepare to celebrate Christmas,
let us join our prayers with those of Mary:
Hail, Mary . . .

In the silence of God's stillness
we name any we know
who specially need our prayer.

Silence

Celebrant
Father, you came to show us the true way to life.
Help us progress along that way in your strength.
Through Jesus Christ, our Lord.
Amen.

SECOND SUNDAY OF ADVENT

*It had been prophesied that there would be a messenger to prepare
the way for the coming of the Messiah. Now John the Baptist
appears with his urgent message of repentance.*

Celebrant
We know that God is here with us,
and hears what is in our thoughts and in our hearts.

Reader
So we pray for all who claim to be Christians
all over the world.
We ask for a real longing for God in our lives;
a longing that is not satisfied by anything else.

Silence

Holy God:
we want to know you better.

We pray for the different countries
and those with power and influence.
We pray for honesty, justice and integrity.

Silence

Holy God:
we want to know you better.

We pray for those we love
and those we find it hard to relate to.
We pray for a deeper, and a loving forgiveness.

Silence

Holy God:
we want to know you better.

We pray for those in pain
and those imprisoned by addiction.
We pray for healing, wholeness and freedom.

Silence

Holy God:
we want to know you better.

We pray for those who have died
and now see God face to face.
We pray for those who miss them here.

Silence

Holy God:
we want to know you better.

Mindful of Mary's quiet
and prayerful acceptance of God's will,
we join our prayers with hers:
Hail, Mary . . .

As we get ready for the coming of his Son,
let us bring to God our Father
our own particular concerns.

Silence

Celebrant
Father, accept these prayers:
as you prepared humanity
for your coming in Bethlehem,
prepare us to receive you in our hearts.
We ask this through Christ our Lord.
Amen.

256

THIRD SUNDAY OF ADVENT

*Our period of preparation shifts from repentance
and forgiveness to the freed exhilaration of hope, as the momentous
truth of God's immanence begins to dawn on us.*

Celebrant
God is here with us now.
Let us pray.

Reader
We want to be ready to receive the Lord.
May he take us as we are and cultivate in us
a heart that longs for and worships the God of love
above and beyond everything else.

Silence

Come, O come:
Emmanuel, God with us.

We open to the Father's love
the spiritual journeys of all who walk the way of Christ;
may they be protected from evil
and kept steadfast in faith.

Silence

Come, O come:
Emmanuel, God with us.

We pray for those who give us support,
and encourage us and listen to us,
and make us laugh and share our sorrows.
May their lives be blessed and filled with joy.

Silence

Come, O come:
Emmanuel, God with us.

We remember in God's presence
those whose memories are painful,

and those whose bitter resentment
cramps and distorts present relationships.
We ask for the healing only God can give.

Silence

Come, O come:
Emmanuel, God with us.

We call to mind those we know who have died,
and any who are close to death at the moment.
As they meet the one true God
may their hearts be opened to receive his love,
mercy and forgiveness.

Silence

Come, O come:
Emmanuel, God with us.

We make our prayer with Mary,
who mothered the Son of God:
Hail, Mary . . .

As the love of God our Father fills our hearts,
we pray for any needs
known to us personally.

Silence

Celebrant
Father, we ask these things
through Jesus Christ our Lord.
Amen.

Fourth Sunday of Advent

When we co-operate with God amazing things happen.

Celebrant
As we share in Mary and Elizabeth's joy
at the coming of our Saviour,
let us quieten and still ourselves
in the presence of God.

Reader
We can only marvel at the way
the heavenly Father is happy to work with us.
We want him to know
that we are willing to be used.

Silence

Let it be to me:
according to your will.

We call to mind those
whom we would love to know the Lord
and we ask that their hearts may be prepared
to recognise him.

Silence

Let it be to me:
according to your will.

We pray for reassurance and encouragement
in this parish
and for insight to the real needs
and what the Lord would have us do.

Silence

Let it be to me:
according to your will.

We ask for the courage
to continue working with and for the Lord,
even during the dark and dangerous times.

Silence

Let it be to me:
according to your will.

We call to mind those who are struggling
with poverty, illness or despair;
may the Lord comfort them
and use us however he wants.

Silence

Let it be to me:
according to your will.

We remember those who have died
and give thanks for the good
that the Lord has worked in their lives.
May we, with them, share in the life
that lasts for ever.

Silence

Let it be to me:
according to your will.

With Mary, the bearer of God's Son,
we make our prayer:
Hail, Mary . . .

We pray to our loving Father,
in silence,
for everything we need.

Silence

Celebrant
In thankfulness we ask you, Father,
to hear our prayers,
through Christ our Lord.
Amen.

CHRISTMAS DAY

*Emmanuel – 'God with us' – is born at Bethlehem
into the human family. Now we will be able to understand,
in human terms, what God is really like.*

Celebrant
As we celebrate God's coming to us
as a human child,
we bring the needs of our world
before the God we can trust.

Reader
We pray for all those who worship God
in every country of our world.
We pray for the grace
to know and love God more deeply.

Silence

Emmanuel, God with us:
we welcome you!

We pray for those who are spending this Christmas
apart from those they love.
We pray for those whose celebrations
are tempered with sorrow or fear.

Silence

Emmanuel, God with us:
we welcome you!

We pray for peace in the Holy Land
and for all who now live in the city of Bethlehem.

Silence

Emmanuel, God with us:
we welcome you!

We pray for those working over Christmas,
for all women giving birth

and all babies being born today.
We pray for their homes and families.

Silence

Emmanuel, God with us:
we welcome you!

We pray for those being born into eternal life
through the gate of death,
and commend them to God's love and mercy.

Silence

Emmanuel, God with us:
we welcome you!

We join our prayers with those of Mary,
who shared her joy with the shepherds:
Hail, Mary . . .

We pray in silence, now,
for our own particular needs and concerns.

Silence

Celebrant
Heavenly Father, accept these prayers
and give us the strength and the will
to walk in love,
through Jesus Christ.
Amen.

FIRST SUNDAY OF CHRISTMAS: THE HOLY FAMILY

Jesus' perception and understanding of his purpose and work begins to take shape throughout his childhood in the Holy Family.

Celebrant
We have been called
to pray for one another in God's presence.
Let us settle ourselves to do that now.

Reader
We pray for all who are called to lead and teach
so that the truth of God's love
is shared throughout the world.
We ask for wisdom, energy
and sensitivity to God's prompting.

Silence

Incarnate God:
we love you and we need you.

We pray for all with power
and influence in our world.
We ask for a widespread desire
for those qualities of compassion and integrity.

Silence

Incarnate God:
we love you and we need you.

We pray for all parents and their children,
especially where there are conflicts,
anxious moments and gaps in communication.

Silence

Incarnate God:
we love you and we need you.

We pray for all missing persons and their families,
all who are rethinking their direction,
all who find life full of contradictions
at the moment.

Silence

Incarnate God:
we love you and we need you.

We pray for those who have come to the end
of their earthly life,
especially any who are unprepared.

Silence

Incarnate God:
we love you and we need you.

We make our prayer with Mary,
Mother of the Church:
Hail, Mary . . .

As members of Christ's family,
we name those we know
who are in any particular need.

Silence

Celebrant
Father, we ask you to hear our prayers,
through Christ our Lord.
Amen.

SECOND SUNDAY OF CHRISTMAS

Christ is the way God tells people about himself.

Celebrant
We have met here
in the real presence of our God.
Let us pray to him now.

Reader
We bring to mind the worldwide Christian Church,
both leaders and people,
as we begin another year.
We ask for a deeper awareness
of God's presence among us.

Silence

Though we cannot see you:
your love surrounds us.

We bring to mind the troubled areas of our world
where corruption, injustice and violence
ruin lives and damage self-worth.
We ask for a renewal of heart and a cleansing grace.

Silence

Though we cannot see you:
your love surrounds us.

We call to mind those we have spent time with
over this Christmas season;
we ask for a blessing upon all our families,
friends and neighbours.

Silence

Though we cannot see you:
your love surrounds us.

We bring to mind all who live away from home,
all refugees and all children in care.
We ask for the security that only the Lord can give.

Silence

Though we cannot see you:
your love surrounds us.

We bring to mind those who have died recently
and all who grieve for them.
We ask for comfort to be given to the dying
and the assurance of the Spirit's presence.

Silence

Though we cannot see you:
your love surrounds us.

We pray with Mary,
who so tenderly nurtured her holy Child:
Hail, Mary . . .

Now, in the space of silence,
we bring to God our Father
our private petitions.

Silence

Celebrant
Heavenly Father,
we ask this through Christ our Lord.
Amen.

THE EPIPHANY OF THE LORD

Jesus, the hope of the nations, is shown to the world.

Celebrant
We are all companions on a spiritual journey.
As we travel together, we pray to God our Father.

Reader
We pray that the worldwide Church
may always be ready
to travel in the Lord's way
and in his direction.

Silence

Light of the world:
shine in our darkness.

We pray for the nations
as they live through conflicts
and struggle with identity.
We long for all peoples
to acknowledge the true and living God.

Silence

Light of the world:
shine in our darkness.

We pray for the families and the streets we represent,
asking for a spirit of generous love,
understanding and mutual respect.

Silence

Light of the world:
shine in our darkness.

We pray for all who are finding their way
tedious, lonely or frightening at the moment;
for those who have lost their way
and do not know what to do for the best.

Silence

Light of the world:
shine in our darkness.

We pray for those who have come
to the end of their earthly journey.

Silence

Light of the world:
shine in our darkness.

We join our prayers with those of Mary,
who showed her Son to the Wise Men:
Hail, Mary . . .

We pray to the Lord, in silence,
for our own needs and cares.

Silence

Celebrant
Father, we commend our lives
to your loving care,
through Christ our Lord.
Amen.

THE BAPTISM OF THE LORD

Jesus is baptised, and God confirms his identity and his calling.

Celebrant
Let us pray to the God
who calls us each by name.

Reader
We pray for all baptised Christians
to live out their calling in loving and holy lives.
We pray for those preparing
for Baptism and Confirmation;
for parents and godparents
to be given the grace and perseverance
to keep faithfully the promises made.

Silence

Come, Holy Spirit:
fill our lives.

We pray for peace and integrity
in all our dealings as individuals,
and in local, national and international conflicts;
for openness to hear God's wisdom
and courage to follow his lead.

Silence

Come, Holy Spirit:
fill our lives.

We pray for harmony and understanding
in our relationships with family and neighbours;
for the willingness both to give and to receive,
for the generosity of forgiving love.

Silence

Come, Holy Spirit:
fill our lives.

We pray for those whose weariness or pain
makes it difficult for them to pray;
may they sense the support and love
of the Church of God.

Silence

Come, Holy Spirit:
fill our lives.

We pray for those whose souls
have left behind their frail and broken bodies
and can now fly freely to live in God's company
for the whole of eternity.
May their loved ones be blessed and comforted
and may we all be brought
to share in the joy of heaven.

Silence

Come, Holy Spirit:
fill our lives.

Now we join our prayers with those of Mary,
the Mother of Jesus:
Hail, Mary . . .

In the silence of God's attentive love,
we name those we know
who are in any particular need.

Silence

Celebrant
Father, confident in your love,
we ask these things
through Christ our Lord.
Amen.

First Sunday of Lent

Following his baptism, Jesus is severely tempted out in the desert,
and shows us how to overcome temptation.

Celebrant
As children of our heavenly Father,
who knows us so well and loves us completely,
let us pray.

Reader
We pray for the Church
as it struggles to steer a straight course
true to the Lord's calling.
We pray for wisdom and courage,
honesty and the willingness to be vulnerable.

Silence

Father, lead us not into temptation:
but deliver us from evil.

Knowing our weakness in the face of temptation,
we ask for strength and protection
so that, though we stumble,
we shall not fall headlong.

Silence

Father, lead us not into temptation:
but deliver us from evil.

We pray for all those
who are fighting temptation
and finding it difficult to resist.
We ask that they may be helped to see clearly,
and be equipped with all they need
to choose what is right.

Silence

Father, lead us not into temptation:
but deliver us from evil.

We pray for those we love,
whose company we enjoy.
We pray too for those who irritate us
and those whom we annoy.

Silence

Father, lead us not into temptation:
but deliver us from evil.

We stand alongside all those who suffer,
all whose lives are in chaos or despair,
and all who live in the dark prison of guilt.
We pray for reassurance and peace,
understanding and compassion.

Silence

Father, lead us not into temptation:
but deliver us from evil.

We pray for the dying,
especially the unnoticed and despised.
We pray for those who have gone through death
and now see the Lord face to face,
that they may receive his merciful forgiveness
and know the joy of living with him for ever.

Silence

Father, lead us not into temptation:
but deliver us from evil.

Now we join our prayers with those of Mary,
the Mother of Jesus:
Hail, Mary . . .

Together in silence,
we name any known to us
with particular needs or burdens.

Silence

Celebrant
Father, we offer you our prayers
in trust and love.
Through Jesus Christ our Lord.
Amen.

SECOND SUNDAY OF LENT

*God's glory transfigures Jesus as he prays on the mountain. Our lives,
too, can become increasingly radiant as the Spirit transforms us.*

Celebrant
As God's people,
let us pray to him now.

Reader
We long to shine with the Lord's light.
May our hearts be set on fire with love for him
and for one another.

Silence

May our lives proclaim:
that the Lord our God is holy.

We pray for lives of light among the darkness
of injustice, corruption and despair;
may those who are already shining
in dark places all over the world
be strengthened.

Silence

May our lives proclaim:
that the Lord our God is holy.

May the Lord come into our homes
and make them places of welcome
where his love is woven
into all our relationships.

Silence

May our lives proclaim:
that the Lord our God is holy.

May those who have to suffer physical pain
or mental and emotional anguish
be given courage and enabled to draw

on the resources of the Spirit
that can transform all our pain and sorrow.

Silence

May our lives proclaim:
that the Lord our God is holy.

May all who have come to the point of death
be welcomed into the kingdom
of everlasting light.
May those who miss their physical presence be comforted,
and may we all be brought to spend eternity
in the radiance of the presence of God.

Silence

May our lives proclaim:
that the Lord our God is holy.

We make our prayer with Mary,
faithful Mother of Jesus:
Hail, Mary . . .

Knowing that God our Father
hears the prayers of his children,
we pray in silence
our own individual petitions.

Silence

Celebrant
Father, we ask all this
through Christ our Lord.
Amen.

THIRD SUNDAY OF LENT

*The great 'I AM' calls people in every generation to repent
so that God's kingdom can be established and grow.*

Celebrant
Remembering the faithfulness of God our Father,
let us pray to him now.

Reader
God our Father is the God of Abraham,
God of Isaac, God of Jacob;
we thank him for his love and faithfulness
in every generation.
We pray for the Church – the community of faith –
for its leaders and teachers, for all the baptised;
may we hear God's word and will for us,
and have the grace to act on it.

Silence

Lead us:
Heavenly Father, lead us.

God our Father is God of the present,
the past and the future;
we pray that his kingdom of love may come
in every place and every heart,
to bring the healing and hope
which he alone can give.

Silence

Lead us:
Heavenly Father, lead us.

May God our Father teach us to be family;
may he be present in our homes,
not reserved for some special place
but in every room and relationship.

Silence

Lead us:
Heavenly Father, lead us.

We pray that the Lord of peace
may anoint the crushed and oppressed
with the balm of his presence,
to uphold and encourage,
to redeem and transform.

Silence

Lead us:
Heavenly Father, lead us.

We commend to the Lord of life
our own loved ones who have died,
in the sure knowledge that death to this life
is not the final end many fear
but the gateway to eternal life.

Silence

Lead us:
Heavenly Father, lead us.

We pray with Mary,
who heard and believed God's promises:
Hail, Mary . . .

In the stillness of our hearts let us pour out
to our listening God
whatever hangs heavily on our hearts
or uplifts us in thankfulness.

Silence

Merciful Father,
we ask you to hear our prayers
which we make through Christ our Lord.
Amen.

FOURTH SUNDAY OF LENT

Be reconciled with God. He is waiting to welcome us.

Celebrant
Gathered together as children in God's family,
let us pray.

Reader
We pray for the insight and discernment we need
in our church community.
May we learn to have a greater love for the Lord
as we learn to live and work in harmony,
focused on him and not on our divisions.

Silence

God our Father:
supply our needs.

Into the unease and weariness of our world
may the Lord pour the reality and wholesome truth we need,
that we may learn mutual trust
and support one another in love.

Silence

God our Father:
supply our needs.

Into the laughter and tears of family life
may the Lord pour the freshness of his living presence,
as we work at our relationships
and deepen our love for one another.

Silence

God our Father:
supply our needs.

Into the loneliness and pain
of those who feel rejected and unvalued
may the Lord pour his compassion and reassurance,

that each person may know
the full extent of his love for them.

Silence

God our Father:
supply our needs.

May the dying know,
and find comfort and hope in the Lord,
and may those who have died in faith
live for ever in the beauty of his holiness.

Silence

God our Father:
supply our needs.

Mary opened her life
to the loving power of God;
we make our prayer with her:
Hail, Mary . . .

We know that our merciful Father hears us;
let us pray in silence now
for our individual needs.

Silence

Celebrant
Father, hear our prayers,
through Christ our Lord.
Amen.

Fifth Sunday of Lent

It is not God's wish to condemn anyone,
but he longs for us to turn to him and live.

Celebrant
God is present with us now.
Let us bring him our prayers and concerns
for the Church and for the world.

Reader
We pray that the loving Lord
may continue to breathe his life into the Church,
so that we may speak his love to the world
and be willing to suffer and prepared for sacrifice.

Silence

Lord, through your love:
transform our lives.

We pray that the loving Lord
may breathe his peace into the world,
so that we may work together co-operatively,
sensitive to one another's needs and differences.

Silence

Lord, through your love:
transform our lives.

We pray that the loving Lord
may breathe his patience and forgiveness
into our homes and all our relationships,
so that we may learn
to cherish and respect one another,
and act with generosity.

Silence

Lord, through your love:
transform our lives.

We pray that the loving Lord
may breathe his encouragement
into every suffering and every sadness,
so that the dark and painful times
become places of strong spiritual growth.

Silence

Lord, through your love:
transform our lives.

We pray that the loving Lord
may breathe his welcome
deep into the souls of the dying,
so that death is only the door
leading to the joy of eternal life.

Silence

Lord, through your love:
transform our lives.

We make our prayer with Mary,
who knew the fullness of God's merciful love:
Hail, Mary . . .

Confident in God's forgiving love,
we pray our personal petitions
to him in silence now.

Silence

Celebrant
Father, accept these prayers,
helping us to follow
your example of forgiveness,
and to love others as you love us.
Through Christ our Lord.
Amen.

Palm (Passion) Sunday

As Jesus rides into Jerusalem on a donkey, and the crowds welcome him,
we sense both the joy at the Messiah being acclaimed, and the heaviness
of his suffering which follows. Jesus' mission is drawing to its fulfilment.

Celebrant
As we recall Jesus entering Jerusalem,
let us gather our thoughts to pray.

Reader
As the crowds welcomed Jesus,
we pray that many more will welcome him
into their hearts and lives over the coming year.
We pray for opportunities to spread the good news
and courage to take them.

Silence

Lord, you are our God:
we welcome you!

We recall the donkey Jesus rode on,
and we pray for that real humility in our hearts
which treats status and image casually,
and truth and loving service seriously.

Silence

Lord, you are our God:
we welcome you!

The children sang and shouted in praise;
we pray for the children in our homes,
our city and our land.
May we not fail them
in the support and teaching they need.

Silence

Lord, you are our God:
we welcome you!

The crowds were responding
to the healing love
they had seen in action in Jesus.
In our love and prayer
we now bring all those we would have brought to Jesus
for healing and help.
May they be given comfort and reassurance,
wholeness and hope.

Silence

Lord, you are our God:
we welcome you!

Jesus knew he was riding to his death.
We pray for all on that last journey,
especially those burdened with fear and guilt.
We commend to God's eternal love all who have died.

Silence

Lord, you are our God:
we welcome you!

We make our prayer with Mary,
who shared her Son's sorrows:
Hail, Mary . . .

Together in silence,
we name those known to us
who need our prayers.

Silence

Celebrant
Father, hear our prayer;
may we praise you not only with our voices
but in the lives we lead.
We ask this through Christ our Lord.
Amen.

EASTER DAY

It is true. Jesus is alive for all time.
The Lord of life cannot be held by death. God's victory over
sin and death means that new life for us is a reality.

Celebrant
With joy in our hearts,
come, let us pray together.

Reader
We remember with gratitude
the presence of the Church
in remote and highly populated areas
all over the world.
We pray for all other Christians rejoicing today
in the wonder of the Resurrection.

Silence

Life-giving God:
give us new life in you.

We pray that we may recognise the risen Lord
as we walk through our days,
and we ask that he may remove anything
which blurs our spiritual vision.

Silence

Life-giving God:
give us new life in you.

We pray for the courage to speak out
against injustice and oppression;
we pray that our leaders may establish and uphold
right values and sensitive legislation.

Silence

Life-giving God:
give us new life in you.

We pray that those of our families and friends
who have not yet met the risen Lord
may be drawn into his company and introduced,
so that they can enjoy his faithfulness and love.

Silence

Life-giving God:
give us new life in you.

We remember those whose lives
are filled with pain, anxiety or sorrow,
and ask that the risen Lord may come alongside them
and speak their name.

Silence

Life-giving God:
give us new life in you.

With the words of Resurrection fresh in our minds,
we commend to the Father's eternal love
those who have died,
that they may live with him for ever.

Silence

Life-giving God:
give us new life in you.

We join our prayers with those of Mary,
in her Easter joy:
Hail, Mary . . .

In and through the power of the risen Lord,
we make our private petitions
and thanksgivings.

Silence

Celebrant
Father, in grateful thanks,
we pray we may be worthy
of all your gifts and blessings.
Hear our prayer through Christ, our risen Lord.
Amen.

SECOND SUNDAY OF EASTER

*Having seen Jesus in person, the disciples are convinced
of the Resurrection. We too can meet him personally.*

Celebrant
In the knowledge that God is here present with us,
let us pray.

Reader
We pray for our bishops, priests and deacons,
in their demanding ministry of love,
that they may be given all the support,
grace and anointing they need.

Silence

Open our eyes, Lord:
to see things your way.

We pray for the gifts of discernment and integrity
among all those who govern, advise and lead.
May all self-centred ambition be cleared away
so that our leaders are free to serve.

Silence

Open our eyes, Lord:
to see things your way.

Whenever we have eye contact with family, friends,
neighbours or colleagues,
we pray that the Lord may be there in that communication,
and remind us of our calling to love one another.

Silence

Open our eyes, Lord:
to see things your way.

We call to mind those whose eyes are wet with tears
or tense with pain.

May they sense the Lord's reassuring love
which can bring us through the darkest of valleys.

Silence

Open our eyes, Lord:
to see things your way.

Jesus is the firstfruit of the new and eternal life.
In gratitude for the privilege
of knowing them here on earth,
we pray for those
who have recently walked through death
into that promise.

Silence

Open our eyes, Lord:
to see things your way.

Together with Mary,
the Mother of our Redeemer,
we make our prayer:
Hail, Mary . . .

In the name of the risen Lord,
we name our own particular cares
and concerns.

Silence

Celebrant
Father, we know that you are here present;
hear the prayers we make,
confident of your love.
Through Christ our Lord.
Amen.

THIRD SUNDAY OF EASTER

Those who know Jesus and recognise that he is the anointed Saviour are commissioned to go out as his witnesses to proclaim the good news.

Celebrant
Let us gather with our prayers
before the God who knows each of us by name.

Reader
We pray for the newly baptised
and those who have recently returned to the Lord.
As the Church, may we support them well
and delight in them as members together
of the Body of Christ.

Silence

Here I am, Lord:
send me!

We pray for strength and protection
against all hypocrisy and double standards
in our society.
We pray for a spirit of genuine service
among all who lead and in all areas
where we have authority.

Silence

Here I am, Lord:
send me!

We pray that our homes and our relationships
may be places where people know,
by the way we look at them and treat them,
that they are valued, cherished
and respected for who they are.

Silence

Here I am, Lord:
send me!

As we call to mind all who have learned
to regard themselves with contempt,
we pray that the Lord may draw near to them
and whisper their true name,
so that they discern the truth
of his love and respect for them.

Silence

Here I am, Lord:
send me!

We pray for the dying
and those who have recently died,
commending them to the joy
and safe-keeping of God's love.

Silence

Here I am, Lord:
send me!

We share Mary's Easter joy
as we join our prayers with hers:
Hail, Mary . . .

In silence filled with love,
we name our particular prayer burdens.

Silence

Celebrant
Father, may we, who confess Christ as Lord,
live in his strength.
Through the same Christ our Lord.
Amen.

Fourth Sunday of Easter

Jesus, the Good Shepherd, leads his flock into eternal life.

Celebrant
As members together of the Body of Christ,
let us pray to the true and living God.

Reader
We pray for the nurture
of each member of the Church;
for the newly baptised and for all
in ordained and lay ministry,
that our love for one another may show
as we work for the coming of the kingdom.

Silence

Direct our hearts, O Lord:
to love you more and more.

We pray for the gift of discernment,
so that we recognise God's presence,
and reverence his face
in the faces of those we meet.

Silence

Direct our hearts, O Lord:
to love you more and more.

We pray for our civil rulers
and all those who govern our country
and make its laws,
that we may act responsibly and with compassion,
attentive to real needs and good values.

Silence

Direct our hearts, O Lord:
to love you more and more.

We pray particularly for homes
filled with suspicion and envy,

and ask for the healing of old hurts,
together with hope and perseverance
as people set out on paths of reconciliation.

Silence

Direct our hearts, O Lord:
to love you more and more.

We pray for those whose capacity for trust and love
has been damaged by other people's sin.
We long for the healing and forgiving power of the Spirit,
so that all who are imprisoned by their past
may walk freely with the Lord.

Silence

Direct our hearts, O Lord:
to love you more and more.

We pray for those who have recently passed
through death,
that they may be judged with mercy,
so that, made whole in God's love,
they may know the joy of eternal life.

Silence

Direct our hearts, O Lord:
to love you more and more.

We pray with Mary,
Mother of the Good Shepherd:
Hail, Mary . . .

In a time of silence,
we share with God our Father
our personal burdens, joys and sorrows.

Silence

Celebrant
Father, hear our prayer;
in joy may we follow the way of Christ,
who alone has the words of eternal life.
Through the same Christ our Lord.
Amen.

FIFTH SUNDAY OF EASTER

*Christ, breaking through the barrier of sin and death, allows us to break
into an entirely new way of living which continues into eternity.*

Celebrant
It is God's love that has drawn us here together.
Let us pray to him now.

Reader
Wherever Christians are fussing and arguing,
living outside the Father's will,
we pray for a deep cleansing, healing and renewing,
so that we may truly be the Body of Christ in our world.

Silence

Lord, you show us:
what loving really means.

Wherever injustice stifles human growth,
and selfish ambition distorts leadership,
we pray for right and good government
throughout the world,
born of wisdom and humility.

Silence

Lord, you show us:
what loving really means.

As we watch our children growing,
may they learn from our example
to grow more loving
in the ways we deal with conflict,
approach difficulties,
and address the needs of those we meet.

Silence

Lord, you show us:
what loving really means.

In the places of long-term pain
and sudden shock,
of weariness, disappointment and fear,
we pray for peace which only God can give
and the comfort which speaks of hope.

Silence

Lord, you show us:
what loving really means.

May the physical death of those we now recall
be nothing less than the gateway
to a new and lasting life in God's love and protection.

Silence

Lord, you show us:
what loving really means.

We join our prayers with those of Mary,
whose life was guided by love:
Hail, Mary . . .

In silence,
we make our private petitions to God,
who knows all our needs.

Silence

Celebrant
Father, confident in your boundless love,
we place these prayers before you.
Through Christ our Lord.
Amen.

SIXTH SUNDAY OF EASTER

The continuing presence of God, as Holy Spirit, leads us,
as Jesus promised, into a personally guided outreach to all nations.

Celebrant
Drawn by the Holy Spirit,
we have arrived at this moment,
when we can pray together for the Church
and for the world.

Reader
As members of the Church in this generation,
we ask for guidance and blessing
for all our deacons, priests and bishops,
and all in training for lay and ordained ministry.
As the people of God, we ask for the gifts we need
for the work we are called to do.

Silence

Lord, you are with us:
every step of the way.

This fragile, vulnerable planet is so beautiful,
and in such need of guidance;
we pray for a deeper valuing
of our universe and of one another;
for the kingdom to come on earth as in heaven.

Silence

Lord, you are with us:
every step of the way.

May our homes be centres of love,
acceptance and welcome;
we pray that the Spirit will make his home among us
in each room and each relationship.

Silence

Lord, you are with us:
every step of the way.

We pray for all who are weighed down
with doubts, fears and misgivings;
all who are haunted by the past
or scared by the future.
We ask for them awareness of the Spirit's constant presence
and the courage he brings.

Silence

Lord, you are with us:
every step of the way.

As we remember those
whose earthly life has come to an end,
we pray that they, and we in our turn,
may be received into heaven
and live for ever in divine light.

Silence

Lord, you are with us:
every step of the way.

We make our prayer with Mary,
tranquil Mother of Jesus:
Hail, Mary . . .

Upheld by God's peace,
we pray now in silence
for any needs known to us personally.

Silence

Celebrant
Heavenly Father, accept our prayers
through Christ our Lord.
Amen.

THE ASCENSION OF THE LORD

Having bought back our freedom with the giving of his life,
Jesus enters into the full glory to which he is entitled.

Celebrant
As we celebrate together, let us pray together.

Reader
As we celebrate this festival
of Jesus' entry into heaven as Saviour and Lord,
we pray for unity in the Church
and reconciliation and renewed vision.

Silence

God of love, both heaven and earth:
are full of your glory.

We pray that the God of our making
may draw us deeper
into the meaning of life.

Silence

God of love, both heaven and earth:
are full of your glory.

We pray for all farewells and homecomings
among our families and in our community,
and for all who have lost touch with loved ones
and long for reunion.

Silence

God of love, both heaven and earth:
are full of your glory.

We pray for those who are full of tears,
and cannot imagine being happy again;
we pray for the hardened and callous,
whose inner hurts have never yet been healed.
We pray for wholeness and comfort and new life.

Silence

God of love, both heaven and earth:
are full of your glory.

We commend to God's eternal love
those we remember who have died,
and we pray too for those
who miss their physical presence.

Silence

God of love, both heaven and earth:
are full of your glory.

We make our prayer with Mary,
sharing her joy at her Son's Ascension:
Hail, Mary . . .

We pray in silence, now,
for our own particular needs and concerns.

Silence

Celebrant
Father, accept our prayers;
fit us for heaven,
to live with you for ever.
Through Christ our Lord.
Amen.

SEVENTH SUNDAY OF EASTER

Jesus lives for all time in glory; we can live the
fullness of Resurrection life straightaway.

Celebrant
Let us pray to the God who gives us so much
and loves us so completely.

Reader
We pray for a fresh outpouring of the Spirit
in all areas of the Church,
till our lives are so changed for good
that people notice and are drawn to the Lord.

Silence

We are your people:
and you are our God.

We pray for godly leaders and advisers
all over the world,
and for the courage to speak out
against injustice and evil.

Silence

We are your people:
and you are our God.

We pray for those affected
by our behaviour and our conversation,
that we may in future
encourage one another by all we say and do.

Silence

We are your people:
and you are our God.

We pray for those as yet unborn,
that the good news will reach them too;
we pray for those who have rejected God

because of the behaviour of his followers;
we pray for all who have lost their way.

Silence

We are your people:
and you are our God.

We pray for the dying,
especially those who are unprepared or frightened.
May all who have died in faith
be welcomed into the kingdom.

Silence

We are your people:
and you are our God.

We join our prayers with those of Mary,
who was filled with the Holy Spirit:
Hail, Mary . . .

In silence, we pray to the Lord
for our own intentions.

Silence

Celebrant
Father, trusting in your love
we lay these prayers before you
through Christ, our Lord.
Amen.

Pentecost

*As Jesus promised, the Holy Spirit is poured out
on the apostles and the Church is born.*

Celebrant
As the Spirit enables us,
let us gather ourselves to pray.

Reader
May all Church leaders,
ordained ministers and the laity
be filled to overflowing
with love for all God's people,
and kindled with fresh zeal
for spreading the good news of the Gospel.

Silence

Spirit of the living God:
fall afresh on us.

May all those negotiating for peace
in the delicate areas of national conflict,
industrial disputes and entrenched bitterness,
be blessed with the peace of God,
tranquil and patient beneath the pressures.

Silence

Spirit of the living God:
fall afresh on us.

In our homes and places of work,
our schools and hospitals,
may there always be time
for the warmth of loving concern
and the comfort of being valued.

Silence

Spirit of the living God:
fall afresh on us.

May all rescue workers be strengthened and kept safe;
may all who are trapped in damaged bodies or minds,
in poverty or tyranny, in earthquakes, floods or storms,
be brought to freedom and safety
and be aware of God's love for them.

Silence

Spirit of the living God:
fall afresh on us.

We pray for those who have died
and all who mourn their going;
may the fears of the dying be calmed.

Silence

Spirit of the living God:
fall afresh on us.

The Holy Spirit came down on Mary,
and with her we pray:
Hail, Mary . . .

Alive to the Holy Spirit,
we name those we know
who are in any particular need.

Silence

Celebrant
Father, accept these prayers
through Christ our Lord.
Amen.

TRINITY SUNDAY

The unique nature of God is celebrated today,
as we reflect on the truth that God is Creator,
Redeemer and Life-giver.

Celebrant
Let us pray to the Father,
in the power of the Holy Spirit,
through Jesus, the Son.

Reader
We pray for all theologians
and those who teach the faith
throughout the Church.
We pray for godly wisdom and human insight.

Silence

Holy God:
help us to know you more.

We pray for peace and co-operation,
harmony and mutual respect
in all our dealings with one another
locally, nationally and internationally.

Silence

Holy God:
help us to know you more.

We pray for those who depend on us,
and those on whom we depend,
for our physical and spiritual needs.
May we be enabled to honour one another
as children of God's making.

Silence

Holy God:
help us to know you more.

We pray for those who feel fragmented;
and for those forced to live apart from loved ones
through war, political unrest,
natural disasters or poverty.
We commend their pain
to the comforting of the Spirit.

Silence

Holy God:
help us to know you more.

We remember those who told us of God
through their words and lives;
we think of those who have died in faith
and ask that we may share with them
the joy of God's presence for ever.

Silence

Holy God:
help us to know you more.

Joining Mary, the Mother of our Lord,
we make our prayer:
Hail, Mary . . .

We pray in silence
to our heavenly Father
for our own personal intentions.

Silence

Celebrant
God our Father, hear our prayer;
may we be led by the Spirit
to a deeper knowledge of you.
Through Christ our Lord.
Amen.

CORPUS CHRISTI

Jesus is the Living Bread, who brings us
eternal life through Communion with him.

Celebrant
Gathered as the Body of Christ,
let us pray together to our heavenly Father.

Reader
As we celebrate Christ's sacramental presence among us,
we rejoice that we can feed on him
and be nourished with his life.
We pray that the people of God
in every part of the world
may grow in holiness and love.

Silence

Feed us, Father:
with the Living Bread.

We pray for those who know deep spiritual hunger
and for the spiritually complacent;
for a world where loneliness and fear
distrust Christ's promise of hope;
for the kingdom of God to come.

Silence

Feed us, Father:
with the Living Bread.

We pray that through our feeding
the communities we live and work in
may be blessed and nourished;
that our homes may be places of prayer,
and that we may have the courage to be vulnerable.

Silence

Feed us, Father:
with the Living Bread.

We pray for all who receive Communion
in hospital or in their own homes;
that they may find strength and healing
through encountering Christ's love.

Silence

Feed us, Father:
with the Living Bread.

We pray for those whose earthly lives
have come to an end,
that in God's eternity they may find
lasting peace and joy.

Silence

Feed us, Father:
with the Living Bread.

We make our prayers with Mary,
who brought the Living Bread into the world:
Hail, Mary . . .

Let us be still in the presence of God
and bring to him the needs and concerns
that weigh on our hearts.

Silence

Celebrant
Heavenly Father,
you nourish us by the body and blood of Jesus,
so that we can share the life of heaven,
both now and at the end of time.
Hear our prayers and provide for us all.
Amen.

SECOND SUNDAY OF THE YEAR

*As a marriage celebrates the beginning of a changed, new life for
the bride and groom, so our loving, faithful God has chosen us
and is ready to transform our lives for the good of the world.*

Celebrant
Drawn by God's love and constant faithfulness to us,
let us pray.

Reader
We pray for all those who would love to believe
but cannot yet trust in the living God.
We pray for those who have rejected God
because of the unloving behaviour of his followers.

Silence

Fill us, Lord:
fill us to the brim.

We pray for all who give orders
and have influence over other people.
We pray that all peoples may be led justly
and with sensitivity.

Silence

Fill us, Lord:
fill us to the brim.

We pray for all our relationships
which need God's transforming love;
we pray for those we irritate and upset
and those who have hurt and upset us.

Silence

Fill us, Lord:
fill us to the brim.

We pray for those whose lives feel empty
and lacking real meaning.
We pray for those whose frailty, pain or illness
makes it difficult to pray.

Silence

Fill us, Lord:
fill us to the brim.

We pray for those who are dying
and those who have completed their life on earth,
that they may be brought to peace
and everlasting joy.

Silence

Fill us, Lord:
fill us to the brim.

We join our prayers with those of Mary,
chosen Mother of our Lord:
Hail, Mary . . .

In silence,
as God our Father listens with love,
we name our own particular cares and concerns.

Silence

Celebrant
God our Father, hear our prayer;
may the richness of your transforming Spirit
refresh and renew our lives.
Through Christ our Lord.
Amen.

THIRD SUNDAY OF THE YEAR

The meaning of the scriptures is revealed to the people.

Celebrant
Let us still our bodies and our minds
as we pray together to the Father.

Reader
As we call to mind
that we are members of the worldwide Church,
we pray for those who are insulted
or persecuted for our shared faith.
We stand alongside them now.

Silence

Open our ears, Lord:
and teach us to listen to you.

We pray that all of us
who inhabit planet Earth in this age
may learn to hear again
and respond to God's voice of creative love.

Silence

Open our ears, Lord:
and teach us to listen to you.

We pray that wherever materialism
or stress or sorrow or sin
have deafened us to God's will,
we may be prompted to put things right.

Silence

Open our ears, Lord:
and teach us to listen to you.

We pray that our homes may be places
where the Lord is welcomed and recognised
through the good and the troubled times.

Silence

Open our ears, Lord:
and teach us to listen to you.

We pray for all who are ill, injured or sad.
May the Spirit show us how we can help,
and give them a real sense
of his comforting presence.

Silence

Open our ears, Lord:
and teach us to listen to you.

We remember those who have travelled through life
and now have gone through death into eternity.
We give thanks for their lives
and commend them to the Lord's safekeeping.
May he prepare us all, through our living, for eternal life.

Silence

Open our ears, Lord:
and teach us to listen to you.

We pray with Mary,
Mother of the Church:
Hail, Mary . . .

We make our own personal petitions
in silence, now,
to God our loving Father.

Silence

Celebrant
Father, we ask you to hear our prayers,
through Christ our Lord.
Amen.

Fourth Sunday of the Year

*As a prophet, Jesus' work is to proclaim the reign of God's love,
not only to the Jewish people but to the whole world.*

Celebrant
Let us pray to our loving and faithful God.

Reader
We pray that the Church may be noticeable by its loving;
that all Christians may be remarkable
for their caring and joyful serving
without restrictions or boundaries.

Silence

Loving Father:
hear our prayer.

We pray that through the power of love
conflicts may be resolved, injustices righted,
corruption cleansed and revenge dissolved,
for the world's healing.

Silence

Loving Father:
hear our prayer.

We pray that our homes may be training grounds
for the selfless loving which gives and forgives,
and never ends.

Silence

Loving Father:
hear our prayer.

We pray that fears may be calmed
and the anxious reassured;
that all in pain may be comforted
and restored to wholeness.

Silence

Loving Father:
hear our prayer.

We pray that through Christ's deathless love
those who have died may be forgiven
and brought to eternal life.

Silence

Loving Father:
hear our prayer.

Encouraged by Mary's example of love,
we join our prayers with hers:
Hail, Mary . . .

In the silence of God's attentive love,
we name those we know
who are in any particular need.

Silence

Celebrant
God our Father, hear these prayers;
give us all those qualities of faith, hope and love
which last for ever.
Through Christ our Lord.
Amen.

FIFTH SUNDAY OF THE YEAR

God calls his people and commissions them.

Celebrant
Let us pray together in the presence of our God.

Reader
We pray for all who have been called
to be workers in God's harvest,
searching for the lost and loving them
into the kingdom.
We pray for those who teach God's love,
both by word and by the way they live.

Silence

Here I am, Lord:
ready for your service!

We pray for those in authority
and in positions of power,
that under their leadership
there may be mutual respect, integrity and justice.
We pray for discernment
to see where injustice needs righting
and when we need to speak out.

Silence

Here I am, Lord:
ready for your service!

We pray for families suffering poverty
or financial difficulties,
for families full of tension and disagreement,
and for families coping with grief or separation.
We pray for the extended families represented here.
We pray for better awareness
of how our behaviour affects others.

Silence

Here I am, Lord:
ready for your service!

We pray for those who have been working all night
and all who work long hours in poor conditions.
We pray for those who have no work
and feel rejected.
We pray for any resisting
what God is calling them into.

Silence

Here I am, Lord:
ready for your service!

We pray for those who have died
and those who grieve for the loss of their company.
We ask for the opportunity to prepare for death
by the way we live from now on.

Silence

Here I am, Lord:
ready for your service!

Remembering Mary's special vocation,
we join our prayer with hers:
Hail, Mary . . .

As God's stillness fills our hearts,
we pray for any needs
known to us personally.

Silence

Celebrant
Heavenly Father, hear us,
give us strength and dedication
to offer ourselves to do his will.
Through Christ our Lord.
Amen.

Sixth Sunday of the Year

The challenges and rewards of living by faith.

Celebrant
Knowing our need of God,
let us pray.

Reader
We bring to mind our Church
both here in *(name of town)* and throughout the world.
It is for right values and right priorities
that we pray, in all we decide and do.

Silence

Lord our God:
in you we put our trust.

We bring to mind all who lead and govern,
and all meetings where important decisions are made.
We pray that justice and mercy are upheld
in line with the Father's loving will.

Silence

Lord our God:
in you we put our trust.

We bring to mind our circle of family and friends
with whom we share the good
and the difficult times.
We pray for the grace to discern more readily
the good in each person
and the gifts they have to offer.

Silence

Lord our God:
in you we put our trust.

We bring to mind those caught up
in the frenetic pressures of life,

and those who are stressed to breaking point.
We pray for insight and courage to change things.

Silence

Lord our God:
in you we put our trust.

We bring to mind the dying,
especially those who are alone,
and we remember those we know who have died.
May they and we share
in the everlasting joy of God's presence.

Silence

Lord our God:
in you we put our trust.

We make our prayer with Mary,
whose trust in the Lord is our example:
Hail, Mary . . .

Together now in silence,
we pray our individual petitions
to our heavenly Father.

Silence

Celebrant
We commend all our cares
to the God who loves us as his children.
Through Christ our Lord.
Amen.

SEVENTH SUNDAY OF THE YEAR

*Jesus teaches us to love our enemies
and forgive those who sin against us.*

Celebrant
God remembers our frailty;
let us pray to him now.

Reader
When conflicts threaten to disrupt our fellowship
in the church community,
may the Spirit help us to deal
with our frustrations and anger,
and give us the grace to forgive.

Silence

Father, may we love one another:
as you have loved us.

When the luggage we carry from the past
interferes with our capacity to cope with the present,
may the Spirit heal the damage from our memories
and transform our experiences for good.

Silence

Father, may we love one another:
as you have loved us.

When the differences in cultures
block our understanding of one another
and obstruct the peace process,
may the Spirit broaden our vision
to discern the common ground.

Silence

Father, may we love one another:
as you have loved us.

When the layers of resentment
have turned into rock,
may the Spirit dissolve them
with the rain of loving mercy.

Silence

Father, may we love one another:
as you have loved us.

As those we have known and loved
pass through the gate of death,
may the Lord have mercy on them,
and receive them into the joy of eternal life.

Silence

Father, may we love one another:
as you have loved us.

We join our prayers with those of Mary,
the Mother of our Lord:
Hail, Mary . . .

We pray in silence now
for our own petitions
to God our heavenly Father.

Silence

Celebrant
Father, accept these prayers;
may your love strengthen
and encourage us all.
Through Christ our Lord.
Amen.

Eighth Sunday of the Year

What we think important flows out in the way we speak.

Celebrant
Let us pray to the God
who knows us as we really are
and loves us so much.

Reader
We bring to the Lord
our desire to see him more clearly
and be more honest with him.
We pray that, as members of his Church,
we may be a people of integrity.

Silence

Open our eyes, Lord:
Heal us from blindness.

We grieve with the oppressed and downtrodden,
we long for Christ to govern the nations,
to soften hardened hearts,
to transform our world with his love.

Silence

Open our eyes, Lord:
Heal us from blindness.

We lay before the Lord
all our relationships,
both the fulfilling and the challenging.

Silence

Open our eyes, Lord:
Heal us from blindness.

We remember with affection and love
those who are in pain or distress,
offering our availability for the Lord to use.
We remember any we have hurt

by our words or attitude,
and ask for the courage and wisdom
to help us put things right.

Silence

Open our eyes, Lord:
Heal us from blindness.

We call to mind those
whom death has hidden from our eyes,
but whom we continue to love and cherish,
knowing they are safe in the Father's care.

Silence

Open our eyes, Lord:
Heal us from blindness.

With Mary, the bearer of God's Son,
we make our prayer:
Hail, Mary . . .

In silence now,
we name any known to us
with particular needs or burdens.

Silence

Celebrant
God our Father,
in our weakness may we rely
on your constant and almighty strength.
We ask you to hear our prayer,
through Christ our Lord.
Amen.

NINTH SUNDAY OF THE YEAR

The good news we have been given is not
just for us, but to pass on to the rest of the world.

Celebrant
We have gathered here today
in the company of the true God.
Let us pray to him now.

Reader
We pray for the Lord's blessing and anointing
on all involved with mission and outreach,
both here and abroad, among children and adults,
as they commit themselves
to spreading the good news.

Silence

You are the living God:
let your will be done in us.

We pray for all who have influence and authority,
through their political standing, fame or wealth;
speak into their hearts of righteousness and justice,
integrity and compassion.

Silence

You are the living God:
let your will be done in us.

We pray that we may take seriously
our responsibilities for nurturing our children
and those who do not yet know God's love.
May our living be transformed to reveal that love.

Silence

You are the living God:
let your will be done in us.

We call to mind those in need
of comfort and reassurance,
all in pain and mental anguish.
We pray for the lapsed and the doubting
and those who need the good news this week.

Silence

You are the living God:
let your will be done in us.

We pray for those who have recently died
and those on that last journey now.
May we all be brought safely to heaven.

Silence

You are the living God:
let your will be done in us.

With Mary, Mother of Jesus,
let us pray:
Hail, Mary . . .

In silence, we pray our individual petitions
to the Lord of all.

Silence

Celebrant
Heavenly Father, we ask you to hear our prayers,
through Christ our Lord.
Amen.

Tenth Sunday of the Year

Our God is full of compassion;
he hears our crying and it is his nature to rescue us.

Celebrant
Let us bring to the God who loves us
our prayers and concerns for the Church
and the world.

Reader
May the God of compassion
take our hearts of stone
and give us feeling hearts,
so that we as the Church
may be more responsive
to the needs and sorrows around us.

Silence

God of love:
show us the Way.

May the God of wisdom
teach all in authority,
inspire those who lead,
protect each nation from evil,
and further each right decision.

Silence

God of love:
show us the Way.

May the God of tenderness
dwell in our homes
through all the times of joy
and all the heartaches and sadness,
teaching us to show one another
the love he shows to us.

Silence

God of love:
show us the Way.

May the God of wholeness
speak into the despair and loneliness
of all who struggle with life and its troubles;
to reassure, affirm and encourage them,
and alert us to ways we can help.

Silence

God of love:
show us the Way.

May the God of peace
be with the dying,
and welcome those who have died in faith
into the full life of the kingdom.

Silence

God of love:
show us the Way.

We make our prayer with Mary,
Mother of our risen Lord:
Hail, Mary . . .

We know our Father is listening;
in silence we bring to him
our own particular needs or burdens.

Silence

Celebrant
God our Father, hear our prayer
and help us to do your will.
Through Christ our Lord.
Amen.

ELEVENTH SUNDAY OF THE YEAR

*God has the authority and the desire to forgive our
sins completely and set us free from guilt.*

Celebrant
Knowing your love for us, Holy God,
we have come before you to pray together.

Reader
We pray for all who have the care of souls,
and are entrusted with helping others to repentance
and giving them good counsel.
We pray for those called to speak God's values,
whatever the danger and regardless of popularity.

Silence

Work in us, Lord:
work in us for good.

We pray for those who refuse
to allow injustice or evil to go unchallenged;
for all who are under pressure
to behave wrongly
or keep quiet about something
they know to be wrong.

Silence

Work in us, Lord:
work in us for good.

We pray for more loving forgiveness
in all our relationships,
for more self-knowledge,
the grace to recognise where we are in the wrong,
and the courage to seek God's forgiveness.

Silence

Work in us, Lord:
work in us for good.

We pray for all imprisoned by guilt, resentment,
bitterness and self-pity,
that they may come to know
the relief of being forgiven.
We pray for all innocent victims,
that their scars may be completely healed.

Silence

Work in us, Lord:
work in us for good.

We pray for those who have died
unprepared to meet the Lord,
and for all who have died in faith.
May the Lord have mercy on us all.

Silence

Work in us, Lord:
work in us for good.

We make our prayer with Mary,
who listened in loving obedience to God:
Hail, Mary . . .

We pray in silence,
making our own petitions
to God our heavenly Father.

Silence

Celebrant
Father, we ask you to hear our prayers
through your Son, Christ our Lord.
Amen.

Twelfth Sunday of the Year

Following Christ means daily taking up our cross.

Celebrant
As followers of Christ, let us pray.

Reader
When following Christ brings danger,
weariness or suffering,
we pray for courage and strength.

Silence

In the shadow of your wings:
we shall be in safety.

When we watch the violence and selfishness
of a bewildered and fearful world,
we know our desperate need for peace.
May Christ's peace transform our world.

Silence

In the shadow of your wings:
we shall be in safety.

When we struggle in our relationships
and ache for those we love,
we pray for guidance, forgiveness
and the grace to go on forgiving.

Silence

In the shadow of your wings:
we shall be in safety.

We pray that into all the suffering, pain and hunger
which cries out from our humanity,
Christ will bring the refreshment of his healing love.

Silence

In the shadow of your wings:
we shall be in safety.

When those we know and love meet death,
and we must let them go,
may they be welcomed into the kingdom
of the Father's eternal peace.

Silence

In the shadow of your wings:
we shall be in safety.

We pray with Mary,
who shared her Son's sorrows:
Hail, Mary . . .

In silence now,
we share with God our Father
our personal burdens, joys and sorrows.

Silence

Celebrant
Father, hear our prayers;
we ask for mercy,
encouragement and support.
Through Christ our Lord.
Amen.

THIRTEENTH SUNDAY OF THE YEAR

When we are called to follow Jesus,
that means total commitment, with no half-measures.

Celebrant
Holy God, you have called us
to meet and pray together,
and here we are.

Reader
We pray for those called
to lay and ordained ministry in the Church,
and for those at present testing their vocation.
We lay before the Lord the work that needs doing here
and ask him to provide people to do it.

Silence

We ask in Jesus' name:
give us grace to discern your answer.

We pray for those called to serve
in positions of authority and influence;
for all leaders to see true greatness as service
and true strength as humility.

Silence

We ask in Jesus' name:
give us grace to discern your answer.

We pray for those called to marriage,
and those called to the single life,
for parents and grandparents,
sons and daughters,
for acceptance of what we cannot change
and strength to live the Christian life
in our present situation.

Silence

We ask in Jesus' name:
give us grace to discern your answer.

We pray for those whose lives
are full of disappointment,
disillusion and discontent;
for all who struggle with great perseverance
in difficult circumstances.
We pray for strength, encouragement and direction.

Silence

We ask in Jesus' name:
give us grace to discern your answer.

We pray for those called, through death,
into eternal life
and freedom from all their pain and suffering.
May they receive mercy
and be welcomed into the kingdom.

Silence

We ask in Jesus' name:
give us grace to discern your answer.

We make our prayer with Mary,
who committed herself fully to God's will:
Hail, Mary . . .

In loving silence, now,
we make our private petitions.

Silence

Celebrant
Lord and heavenly Father,
as we commit our lives afresh to your service,
we ask you to hear our prayers.
Through Christ our Lord.
Amen.

Fourteenth Sunday of the Year

In Christ we become a new creation.

Celebrant
Let us bring our cares and concerns
before the God who loves us.

Reader
We pray for more workers
to gather in the harvest of the kingdom;
for our churches to be places of welcome
and wholesome spiritual nurture.

Silence

Use us, Lord:
in the building of your kingdom.

We pray for our nation and the nations of the world;
for an upholding of godly principles and just laws,
for reconciliation, peace and mutual co-operation.

Silence

Use us, Lord:
in the building of your kingdom.

We pray for those among our families and friends
who have no idea of the new life the Lord offers;
we pray for them to discover him
so they may share the joy of living in his love.

Silence

Use us, Lord:
in the building of your kingdom.

We pray for those who are suffering,
for those disfigured by disease or accidents,
for the lonely, the confused and the outcasts.

Silence

Use us, Lord:
in the building of your kingdom.

We pray for the dying, and their loved ones,
for those who have passed through death,
and the families and friends who miss them.
May they be surrounded by the Father's everlasting love.

Silence

Use us, Lord:
in the building of your kingdom.

We pray now with Mary,
serene Mother of our Lord:
Hail, Mary . . .

God our Father loves us;
in silence we pray
our personal petitions to him now.

Silence

Celebrant
Father, knowing that you alone
have the words of eternal life,
we lay our prayers before you.
Through Christ our Lord.
Amen.

FIFTEENTH SUNDAY OF THE YEAR

Straighten your lives out and live by God's standards of love.

Celebrant
Let us pray to God,
knowing we can trust him.

Reader
We pray that as Christians we may take to heart
the need to walk the talk,
and live out what we profess.
We pray that nothing may get so important to us
that it pushes God's values aside.

Silence

Father:
let only your will be done.

We pray that those in authority and power
do not lose touch with the needs of those they serve,
so that the poor and oppressed and vulnerable
are always given value and respect.

Silence

Father:
let only your will be done.

We pray for those in our families
whom we love and have hurt or upset;
we pray too for those who have hurt or upset us,
and ask for God's reconciliation and healing.

Silence

Father:
let only your will be done.

We pray for those who have lost hope
of being rescued, noticed or valued;

for the complacent who cannot see their poverty,
for the prejudiced who mistake blindness for sight.

Silence

Father:
let only your will be done.

We pray for our loved ones
who have reached the moment of death;
we give thanks for the example of their lives
and commend them all to God's safekeeping.

Silence

Father:
let only your will be done.

Mary's example teaches us
the power of loving response;
with her we make our prayer:
Hail, Mary . . .

In the silence of God's stillness,
we name any we know
who especially need our prayer.

Silence

Celebrant
Lord God of love,
we offer you these prayers,
through Christ our Lord.
Amen.

Sixteenth Sunday of the Year

Attentive listening is all part of serving.

Celebrant
Our God is always ready to listen.
Let us pray to him now.

Reader
We pray to the Lord
that he may continue to pour out his gifts on the Church,
so that many may be saved
and our faith may grow strong
and bear much fruit.

Silence

God of Love:
we put our trust in you.

We pray to the Lord
that he may look with mercy on the conflicts of our world;
that we may realign our values and goals
until they are in line with his will,
and our laws and expectations
reflect his justice and love.

Silence

God of Love:
we put our trust in you.

We pray to the Lord
that he may bless our homes and families
and all our neighbours and friends;
may we listen to one another with full attention,
and recognise one another's gifts.

Silence

God of Love:
we put our trust in you.

We pray to the Lord
that he may encourage the hesitant,

curb the overpowering,
heal the sick, refresh the exhausted,
soften the hardened hearts,
open the eyes of the complacent,
and comfort all who are sad.

Silence

God of Love:
we put our trust in you.

We pray to the Lord
that he may welcome into eternity
all those who have died in faith;
may we in our turn share with them
the joy of living in his peace for ever.

Silence

God of Love:
we put our trust in you.

We pray with Mary,
who was the first to welcome Jesus:
Hail, Mary . . .

In the silence of God's attentive love,
we pray our private petitions.

Silence

Celebrant
God our Father, hear our prayer;
we ask you to help us fix our lives on you.
Through Christ our Lord.
Amen.

SEVENTEENTH SUNDAY OF THE YEAR

*Keep asking for God's Spirit and he will keep
pouring out his blessing on you.*

Celebrant
Heavenly Father, as you have taught us,
through Jesus,
we come to you in prayer.

Reader
We pray for all who uphold and teach the faith,
for young Christians in schools and universities,
for Christians witnessing to their faith at work,
for all in danger of persecution.
We pray for strength and courage.

Silence

In all things, Father:
let your will be done.

We pray for discernment and wisdom
as we strive for international co-operation
in managing the world's resources;
for perseverance as we work
towards peace and reconciliation.

Silence

In all things, Father:
let your will be done.

We pray for the good sense
in our family and community life
that knows the difference
between generosity and indulgence,
between lenience and neglect of responsibility.

Silence

In all things, Father:
let your will be done.

We pray for all victims of abuse and tyranny,
for all who suffer long-term effects
of torture, war or disease;
we pray for the grace to forgive,
and for healing of body, mind and spirit.

Silence

In all things, Father:
let your will be done.

We pray for those who have died,
and particularly for those
who have no one to mourn their going;
for those who have died unnoticed.
We pray that they may rest in peace for ever.

Silence

In all things, Father:
let your will be done.

Mary's response prepared the way
for our salvation;
we make our prayer with her:
Hail, Mary . . .

In silence filled with love,
we name our particular prayer burdens.

Silence

Celebrant
God our Father,
rejoicing in your tenderness and compassion,
we bring these prayers before you.
Through Christ our Lord.
Amen.

EIGHTEENTH SUNDAY OF THE YEAR

True richness is not material wealth;
true security is not a financial matter.

Celebrant
Let us pray to God our Father,
knowing that we are all precious to him.

Reader
We pray for all those who give
to support the work of the Church;
may the Lord bless our giving,
guide our spending,
and help us to value the true wealth
of his abundant love.

Silence

The Lord is our shepherd:
there is nothing we shall want.

We pray for the world's economy;
for fair management and distribution of resources;
for fair trade and just wages;
for greater awareness and concern about injustice;
for a commitment to our responsibilities
as planet-sharers and earth-dwellers.

Silence

The Lord is our shepherd:
there is nothing we shall want.

We pray for all parents with young children;
may they be blessed and guided in their parenting;
we pray for families in debt;
for those whose homes have been repossessed,
and those whose financial security
makes them forgetful of God's love.

Silence

The Lord is our shepherd:
there is nothing we shall want.

We pray for those who are burdened
with financial worries
and all who struggle to make ends meet,
all over the world;
we pray for the emotionally and spiritually bankrupt,
and those who do not yet know God's love for them.

Silence

The Lord is our shepherd:
there is nothing we shall want.

We pray for those who have died,
and those on that last journey at this moment;
for a merciful judgement
and the everlasting joy of heaven.

Silence

The Lord is our shepherd:
there is nothing we shall want.

We pray with Mary,
who knew the true value of all things:
Hail, Mary . . .

In the silence of our hearts,
we bring to our heavenly Father
our needs and concerns.

Silence

Celebrant
Lord our God,
acknowledging your greatness,
we ask you to accept these prayers,
through Christ our Lord.
Amen.

Nineteenth Sunday of the Year

Have faith in God, and get yourself ready to meet him.

Celebrant
As God's beloved children,
let us come to him and open our hearts to him.

Reader
The Father knows both our gifts as a congregation
and the needs of those in this parish;
we ask him to bless our ministry in this place,
to strengthen and encourage all Church leaders
and to deepen our faith and sure hope.

Silence

Lord our God:
we believe and trust in you.

We pray that the Father may heal our nation
and all the nations
of what is in the past and still corrodes the present,
so that we may build on good foundations
and learn to govern ourselves with honesty,
respect for one another and sensitivity to needs.

Silence

Lord our God:
we believe and trust in you.

We pray that the Father may be present
in the daily living of our homes
and in all our relationships,
and make us more trustworthy in our friendships,
and strengthen our resolve to live our faith in action.

Silence

Lord our God:
we believe and trust in you.

We call to mind all whose capacity to trust
has been damaged;
for those who are victims of injustice or corruption;
for the very young and the very old,
the frail, the vulnerable and the bereaved.

Silence

Lord our God:
we believe and trust in you.

We remember those
who have completed their earthly life in faith
and have now seen the Lord face to face.
May they know the peace of eternity;
we too look forward to sharing that life of joy.

Silence

Lord our God:
we believe and trust in you.

We make our prayer with Mary,
who was ever watchful in God's service:
Hail, Mary . . .

We pray in silence
to God, who knows our needs.

Silence

Celebrant
God our Father, accept our prayers;
as we learn to trust more in your promise,
may we grow to be more like Christ
and reflect the radiance of his love.
Through the same Christ, our Lord.
Amen.

TWENTIETH SUNDAY OF THE YEAR

When we fix our eyes on Jesus our lives will reflect his nature.

Celebrant
God is close to us as we pray.
He is attentive to us now.

Reader
Whenever the Lord weeps over our harshness,
may his tears melt our hearts of stone.
Whenever he grieves over our double standards,
may we be shocked into honesty again.
May he make us receptive to his teaching,
willing to take risks
and eager to run with our eyes fixed on him.

Silence

Lead us, Lord:
to walk in your ways.

Whenever the news overwhelms us,
may the Lord nudge us to fervent prayer.
Wherever leaders meet to negotiate peace,
may he be present at the conference table.
May he breathe his values into our thinking,
tear down the divisive barriers
and renew us to lead the world into loving.

Silence

Lead us, Lord:
to walk in your ways.

We pray that whenever tempers are frayed
and patience is wearing thin,
the Spirit may give us space
to collect ourselves and try again.
Whenever the demands of family and friends
remind us of our limitations,
may the Spirit minister graciously through our weakness
and teach us the humility of apologising.

Silence

Lead us, Lord:
to walk in your ways.

Whenever people are enveloped by pain
or desolate grief or total exhaustion,
may the Spirit bring refreshment and peace,
tranquillity and hope,
and wherever the grip of the past
prevents free movement into the future,
bring release and healing.

Silence

Lead us, Lord:
to walk in your ways.

We pray for the dying,
especially those who are fearful and distressed,
may they be comforted and reassured
on that last journey.
May those who care for them
and those who mourn their going be blessed.

Silence

Lead us, Lord:
to walk in your ways.

We make our prayer with Mary,
Mother of our Saviour:
Hail, Mary . . .

Trustingly we pray in silence
to God our Father,
who considers each one of us special.

Silence

Celebrant
Loving Father, hear our prayers,
through Christ our Lord.
Amen.

Twenty-First Sunday of the Year

At the great and final gathering in, it will be a question
of each person's chosen life direction,
and each response to the way of God.

Celebrant
Trusting not in ourselves but in God's mercy,
let us pray.

Reader
That in all the decisions and activities of the church,
we may be slow to rush ahead of God's guiding
yet quick to follow where he leads.

Silence

In you, O Lord:
we place our trust.

That in all the hardships and dangers of life,
in all the crises, conflicts and injustices,
we may keep clear-sighted and attentive to God's will.

Silence

In you, O Lord:
we place our trust.

That with our friends, neighbours and loved ones,
and those we are tempted to despise or dismiss,
we may have many opportunities
for loving service.

Silence

In you, O Lord:
we place our trust.

That in those who live fearfully,
God may breathe his peace,
and on those who are ill and frail,
he may place healing hands.

Silence

In you, O Lord:
we place our trust.

That God's comfort may surround all
who are dying unrecognised or unnoticed,
and that all who die in God's friendship
may be welcomed into eternity with him.

Silence

In you, O Lord:
we place our trust.

We join our prayers with those of Mary,
our spiritual Mother:
Hail, Mary . . .

Confident in God's welcoming love,
we pray in silence now,
for our own particular needs and concerns.

Silence

Celebrant
God our Father, accept these prayers,
through Christ our Lord.
Amen.

Twenty-second Sunday of the Year

*When we live God's way, both individually
and as a community, we will be greatly blessed.*

Celebrant
Let us do the work of prayer
that God has asked of us.

Reader
As the body constantly breathes,
may the Church, the body of Christ, constantly pray,
breathing God's life into all its members and activities.

Silence

The Lord is our helper:
we shall not be afraid.

As a new week begins in our world,
may wrong priorities be challenged and adjusted,
may our societies reflect God's concern
for righteousness, true justice and responsive love,
and may all leaders grow in humility,
attentive to the needs of those they serve.

Silence

The Lord is our helper:
we shall not be afraid.

As we call to mind our loved ones,
all who depend on us,
and those on whom we depend,
all with whom we laugh, cry, work or play,
cleanse and refresh our relationships
and give us greater love,
understanding and forgiveness.

Silence

The Lord is our helper:
we shall not be afraid.

We think of those who are in prison,
locked in cells or depression or dysfunctional bodies;
we think of those in hospital wards
and accident centres,
those unable to reach medical help
and those on long waiting-lists for operations;
as we think of them all, we pray for them all.

Silence

The Lord is our helper:
we shall not be afraid.

We remember the dying and those who love them;
we remember those whose earthly life
has come to an end,
and we commend them to God's undying love.

Silence

The Lord is our helper:
we shall not be afraid.

Mindful of Mary's quiet
and prayerful acceptance of God's will,
we join our prayers with hers:
Hail, Mary . . .

In silence, we pray for our own intentions
to God, our loving Father.

Silence

Celebrant
Lord God, giver of all good gifts,
we ask you to hear these prayers.
Through Christ our Lord.
Amen.

Twenty-Third Sunday of the Year

Following Jesus is expensive –
it costs everything, but it's worth it.

Celebrant
Let us pray to the God who has watched our growing
throughout our lives, and loves us.

Reader
There is nothing hidden from the Lord.
All our thoughts and plans and secret fears
are open to him, even when we try to hide them.
May he give us the courage and strength
to deal with the doubts and misgivings
and fears of his Church,
with the love and mercy
which are part of his nature.

Silence

Gracious God:
in you we can trust.

The Lord feels for the oppressed and the forgotten;
understands the damage which can lead to violence,
the insecurity which can lead to defensiveness,
and the neglect which can lead to lack of control.
We pray that he may heal the nations,
restore what has been lost,
and turn our hearts to discern his will.

Silence

Gracious God:
in you we can trust.

The Lord knows the love inside our hearts for one another
that sings and dances and aches and worries.
We pray that the Spirit may work on us now
in the depth of our being,
and bless our loved ones with a sense of joy.

Silence

Gracious God:
in you we can trust.

The Lord suffers with those who suffer
and weeps with those who weep;
we, too, stand alongside them now
in whatever pain, distress or sorrow
is engulfing them,
and we pray that they may be comforted.

Silence

Gracious God:
in you we can trust.

The Lord's death and resurrection
proclaim the message of hope
amongst the tears of our grieving
for those who have died.
May they be welcomed
into the eternal light of the kingdom.

Silence

Gracious God:
in you we can trust.

We join our prayers with those of Mary,
who spent her life in God's service:
Hail, Mary . . .

In silence, we make our own petitions
to God, who loves us as his own.

Silence

Celebrant
Father, accept our prayers;
all that we are,
and all we are capable of becoming,
we pledge to your service.
Through Christ our Lord.
Amen.

TWENTY-FOURTH SUNDAY OF THE YEAR

Jesus does not avoid the company of sinners but befriends them.

Celebrant
Let us pray to the God who longs for all to be rescued.

Reader
We pray for our bishops, priests and deacons,
and all who are called
to the different ministries in the Church.
May they be blessed
as they work in the service of the Lord.

Silence

God our shepherd:
all our needs are known to you.

We pray for all peace initiatives
and every genuine attempt at negotiation
in conflict resolution.
May those who govern be governed by the Father's love;
may those who lead be led by the Spirit's directing;
may the whole world come to know its need of Christ.

Silence

God our shepherd:
all our needs are known to you.

We pray for our families and friends,
for those we meet each day and those we seldom see;
may all our loved ones be drawn closer to the Lord.
May he search out those whose faith
is fragile or fragmented.

Silence

God our shepherd:
all our needs are known to you.

As we recall the needs
of those who are sad or lonely,
lost, or afraid of what they have become,
we pray for the knowledge of the Father's love
to wrap warmly around them,
and his living presence
to bring them to a place of safety and hope.

Silence

God our shepherd:
all our needs are known to you.

We pray for those who have recently died;
may they enjoy the eternal life of heaven,
where there is no more pain, sorrow or weariness,
and every tear shall be wiped away.

Silence

God our shepherd:
all our needs are known to you.

We join our prayers with those of Mary,
Mother of our forgiving Lord:
Hail, Mary . . .

Together in silence,
we name those known to us
who especially need our prayer.

Silence

Celebrant
Merciful Father, accept these prayers,
through Christ our Lord.
Amen.

TWENTY-FIFTH
SUNDAY OF THE YEAR

If you cannot be trusted with worldly riches,
or even small amounts of money, then you will
not be trusted with spiritual riches either.

Celebrant
As God has taught us, let us pray
for the coming of the kingdom in every situation.

Reader
We pray for the Church to be pure and holy,
alight with God's love and compassion,
and free from behaviour which is unworthy
of God's chosen people.

Silence

God our Father:
let your kingdom come.

We pray for the nations to be wisely governed,
with just laws and a sense of vision
which reflects the best of human nature.
We pray for peace and mutual respect
in each community throughout the world.

Silence

God our Father:
let your kingdom come.

We pray for our homes to be filled with God's love,
so we are happy to put ourselves out for others,
to listen with full attention, and to value one another.
We pray for the strength
to clear away anything in our life-style
which competes with God for our commitment.

Silence

God our Father:
let your kingdom come.

We pray for those who feel neglected
or rejected by society,
that they may know God's love and acceptance of them.
We pray for all those in pain and distress,
that they may be comforted and relieved.

Silence

God our Father:
let your kingdom come.

We pray that the dying may recognise
their need of God and his power to save;
that those who have died may be judged with mercy
and rest in God's peace.

Silence

God our Father:
let your kingdom come.

We pray with Mary, Mother of Jesus:
Hail, Mary . . .

In silence, now,
we pour out to God our Father
any needs and burdens known to us personally.

Silence

Celebrant
Lord God of all creation,
accept these prayers,
through Christ our Lord.
Amen.

TWENTY-SIXTH
SUNDAY OF THE YEAR

*Wealth can make us complacent so that we fail
to notice the needs of those around us.*

Celebrant
All our needs are God's concerns.
Let us pray to him now.

Reader
May we be a listening Church,
welcoming to the hesitant,
encouraging to the young,
sensitive to the differences and attentive to the needs.

Silence

God, in mercy:
hear us as we pray.

May we be a caring world,
wise in government,
honest in promises,
far-sighted in the management of resources,
and open-hearted in charitable giving.

Silence

God, in mercy:
hear us as we pray.

May we be a responsible community,
supporting our neighbours and friends,
sharing one another's sorrows and joys,
and opening our homes to the presence of the Lord.

Silence

God, in mercy:
hear us as we pray.

As we remember those
who have asked for our prayers,
we ask that the Lord may take their needs
and provide for them,
take their wounds and heal them,
take their suffering and comfort them.

Silence

God, in mercy:
hear us as we pray.

As we call to mind those who have died,
may they know the welcoming of God's love
into eternal joy.

Silence

God, in mercy:
hear us as we pray.

We make our prayer with Mary,
whose generous heart
was so open to God's will:
Hail, Mary . . .

In silence, let us commend
our own particular needs and thankfulness
to the God of power and mercy.

Silence

Celebrant
Heavenly Father, hear these prayers,
through your Son, Jesus Christ.
Amen.

TWENTY-SEVENTH
SUNDAY OF THE YEAR

God hears our distress and our crying, and feels it with us.

Celebrant
Knowing that God hears our prayers,
let us share our concerns with him
for the Church and for the world.

Reader
We pray for all in lay and ordained ministry,
as they labour for the growth
of God's kingdom on earth;
may he keep them strong in the faith,
provide them with the energy and resources they need,
and inspire them daily with his love.

Silence

Lord, you are our hope:
you are our strength.

We pray for all meetings, conventions,
and conferences,
for all policy making and planning;
may delicate negotiations be sensitively led,
and painful decisions bravely and wisely taken.

Silence

Lord, you are our hope:
you are our strength.

We pray for those we have upset or angered,
and those who have upset or angered us;
we pray for those who worry us,
and those we love but seldom manage to see.

Silence

Lord, you are our hope:
you are our strength.

We pray for those who are far from home
and those for whom it is too dangerous
to return home;
we pray for the lonely, the unhappy,
those in pain and those convalescing.

Silence

Lord, you are our hope:
you are our strength.

We remember those who have come
to the end of their earthly life,
and for those whose lives feel bleak
and empty without them.
We pray for mercy and peace and comfort.

Silence

Lord, you are our hope:
you are our strength.

We pray with Mary,
whose faith was unfaltering:
Hail, Mary . . .

Trustingly we pray in silence
to our loving God for our own needs and cares.

Silence

Celebrant
Father, as we dedicate ourselves afresh
to serving you,
accept these prayers,
through Christ our Lord.
Amen.

Twenty-eighth Sunday of the Year

God can always use even seemingly hopeless situations for good.

Celebrant
God has proclaimed his love for us.
We can trust him with all our cares and concerns.

Reader
We pray that the Church may be healed
of all its splits and divisions,
and grow towards unity.

Silence

Have pity on us, Lord:
you alone can save us.

May our society be mindful of those
who have particular difficulties;
may our laws testify to our sense of justice,
honour and integrity;
may the world's leaders be wisely advised
and honestly motivated.

Silence

Have pity on us, Lord:
you alone can save us.

May the Lord walk in our homes
with gifts of peace, patience, forgiveness and joy;
may he help us through the disappointments and tragedies,
and celebrate with us in all our festivities,
as our most honoured guest.

Silence

Have pity on us, Lord:
you alone can save us.

We pray for all suffering from leprosy
and other infectious and life-threatening diseases;
may the Lord give courage
to the long-term and chronically ill,
and respite to those who are at their wits' end.

Silence

Have pity on us, Lord:
you alone can save us.

We remember those who have died,
and we think of their loved ones, who miss them.
May this earthly death be a birth
into the eternal joy of heaven.

Silence

Have pity on us, Lord:
you alone can save us.

We make our prayer with Mary,
whose heart was full of thanks and praise:
Hail, Mary . . .

Confident in God's welcoming love,
we pray in silence, now,
for any needs known to us personally.

Silence

Celebrant
Heavenly Father, to whom all glory belongs,
accept our prayers, through Christ our Lord.
Amen.

TWENTY-NINTH SUNDAY OF THE YEAR

Don't get side-tracked; always pray and don't give up.

Celebrant
Our help comes from the Lord.
Let us pray to him now.

Reader
We pray for those who teach prayer
and open the Scriptures to others
at schools and colleges, retreat houses,
and conferences,
and in churches and homes all over the world.
We pray that many will find in Scripture
words speaking into their situation
and providing the guidance they need.

Silence

Lord, we love your ways:
our help comes from you.

We pray for those picking their way
through situations of potential conflict and danger;
for law makers and keepers
and all who are oppressed unjustly;
for the leaders of the nations and their people.

Silence

Lord, we love your ways:
our help comes from you.

We pray for the grace to listen to one another
and respond to one another's needs;
we pray for a spirit of co-operation and generosity
in our homes and neighbourhoods.

Silence

Lord, we love your ways:
our help comes from you.

We pray for those who are wrestling with problems
which seem too big to cope with;
for those who have recently received news
that has stunned or appalled them,
and are still in a state of shock.

Silence

Lord, we love your ways:
our help comes from you.

We pray for those who have gone through death,
that they may be judged with mercy
and brought safely into the eternal life of heaven.

Silence

Lord, we love your ways:
our help comes from you.

Encouraged by Mary's prayerful example,
we join our prayer with hers:
Hail, Mary . . .

We pray in silence our own petitions
to God our Father,
who knows all our needs.

Silence

Celebrant
God, our heavenly Father,
bless our lives to your service,
and accept our prayers,
through Christ our Lord.
Amen.

THIRTIETH SUNDAY OF THE YEAR

*When we recognise our dependence on God we will
approach him with true humility and accept his gifts with joy.*

Celebrant
Let us pray to the God who made us and sustains us.

Reader
We pray for the Church,
with all our faults and failings,
missed opportunities and misunderstandings;
may we be guided
to be truly the Body of Christ on earth.

Silence

God of our making:
have mercy on us.

We lay before the Lord the political issues,
the moral dilemmas and the dreams of peace
that concern our world,
and all who share its resources.
Where we can see no clear way forward
we pray for vision to enable us
to be good stewards of all God provides.

Silence

God of our making:
have mercy on us.

We pray that the Lord may take all our relationships
and drench them in his transforming love,
so that we appreciate one another more,
and value what each has to offer.

Silence

God of our making:
have mercy on us.

We pray for those who feel spiritually dried-up
or emotionally drained;
may the Lord heal and mend
broken bodies and broken hearts,
and provide clear pools of water for those
who are walking the valley of misery and depression.

Silence

God of our making:
have mercy on us.

We pray for those who have run the race
and fought the good fight;
may the Lord have mercy
on all who are at the point of death,
and receive them into his kingdom.

Silence

God of our making:
have mercy on us.

May we learn from the humility of Mary,
as we pray with her to the God of heaven:
Hail, Mary . . .

In silence now,
we make our private petitions to God,
who always hears our prayers of faith.

Silence

Celebrant
Lord God, accept these prayers,
through Christ our Lord.
Amen.

THIRTY-FIRST
SUNDAY OF THE YEAR

Jesus came to search out the lost and save them.
Through him we come to our senses and make our lives clean.

Celebrant
Let us still ourselves in our Father's presence
and tell him what is on our hearts.

Reader
We pray that the Lord may look into us and teach us
to know ourselves more honestly,
to recognise the areas which need cleansing,
and inspire us to live more faithfully and fruitfully
as the people of God.

Silence

Lord, may our lives:
express our love for you.

We pray that parliaments and all places of government
throughout the world may be filled
with a desire for integrity and a determination
to stamp out corruption and deceit.

Silence

Lord, may our lives:
express our love for you.

May the Lord speak his peace and reconciliation
into all family disputes
and hurtful misunderstandings;
and may a spirit of loving community
be nurtured in our neighbourhood,
heightening our awareness of one another's needs.

Silence

Lord, may our lives:
express our love for you.

We pray that the Lord may bring
reassurance and practical help
to those who are close to despair
and those in long-term suffering;
may he use us as instruments of his healing love.

Silence

Lord, may our lives:
express our love for you.

We pray for those
who have faithfully lived out their days;
as we miss their physical presence,
may they be brought into the peace
of God's kingdom.

Silence

Lord, may our lives:
express our love for you.

As we join our prayers with those of Mary,
may we learn from her responsive love:
Hail, Mary . . .

In silence, now,
we pour out to God our Father
any needs and burdens
known to us personally.

Silence

Celebrant
Heavenly Father,
trusting in your amazing love,
we ask you to accept these prayers.
Through Christ our Lord.
Amen.

THIRTY-SECOND SUNDAY OF THE YEAR

Life after death is not wishful thinking but a definite reality.

Celebrant
Let us pray to the great God of heaven
who stands among us now.

Reader
We pray that we, the earthly part of the Church,
may always reflect
the living presence of Christ among us,
in our liturgy and in our daily living.

Silence

You are our God:
living for ever and ever.

We pray for guidance in our world
as we work out policies and target needs,
and misunderstand one another's cultures
and get carried away with excesses
and the taste of power.

Silence

You are our God:
living for ever and ever.

We pray that our waking, working, eating,
relaxing and sleeping
may become a pattern coloured and lit by God's love;
may our homes reflect it,
our places of work be energised by it,
and our relationships glow with it.

Silence

You are our God:
living for ever and ever.

To those who are losing heart
we pray that the Lord may give
his heavenly encouragement and patience;
to the young and vulnerable
give his heavenly protection;
to the ill and the damaged
give his heavenly healing and inner peace,
as he touches our lives.

Silence

You are our God:
living for ever and ever.

Knowing that physical death
is not the end of life,
but the beginning of a new dimension,
we recall our loved ones who have died
and commend them to God's eternal keeping.

Silence

You are our God:
living for ever and ever.

We pray now with Mary,
Mother of our risen Lord:
Hail, Mary . . .

God our Father loves us as his children;
together in silence,
we name our personal prayer burdens.

Silence

Celebrant
All-powerful God, accept these prayers,
through Christ our Lord.
Amen.

THIRTY-THIRD
SUNDAY OF THE YEAR

There will be dark and dangerous times
as the end approaches, but by standing firm
through it all we will gain life.

Celebrant
The Lord is always ready to listen;
let us pray to him now.

Reader
We pray particularly for those
whose faith is being battered
and those who no longer pray;
we pray that our faith
may be deepened and strengthened.

Silence

Lord, keep us faithful:
firm to the end.

We pray for those whose responsibility it is
to manage the world's economy,
and for those who have difficult
ethical decisions to make;
we pray for wisdom and courage to do what is right.

Silence

Lord, keep us faithful:
firm to the end.

We pray for the world our children will inherit
and ask blessings on all parents
and the responsibilities they face;
we ask for understanding, maturity,
and the gift of laughter.

Silence

Lord, keep us faithful:
firm to the end.

We pray for the victims of disasters,
famines, earthquakes and plagues;
for all who are crying
and those who have no tears left.
We pray for comfort, renewed strength,
and available friends.

Silence

Lord, keep us faithful:
firm to the end.

We pray for those who are nearing death
and those who have died;
especially we pray for those
who have died suddenly and unprepared.
We pray for mercy and forgiveness.

Silence

Lord, keep us faithful:
firm to the end.

We pray with Mary,
who followed her Son even to Calvary:
Hail, Mary . . .

In silence now,
we make our private petitions to God,
who knows what is in our hearts.

Silence

Celebrant
God our Father,
trusting in your constant care and protection,
we bring you these prayers.
Through Christ our Lord.
Amen.

CHRIST THE KING

This Jesus, dying by crucifixion between criminals,
is the anointed King of all creation in whom all things are reconciled.

Celebrant
Through Jesus, our King, let us pray to God the Father.

Reader
As we celebrate Jesus, the head of the Church body,
we pray for all the members
with their various gifts and ministries;
we pray that even our weaknesses
can be used for the glory of God
and for the good of the world.

Silence

Christ is the image:
of the invisible God we worship.

May all monarchs and heads of state
be led in ways of truth and righteousness,
and recognise with humility
that they are called to serve.
We pray for all shepherds,
rescue teams and trouble-shooters;
for all who work to recover the lost.

Silence

Christ is the image:
of the invisible God we worship.

May we reach out to one another
with greater love and better understanding;
we pray for our homes, our relatives,
our neighbours and our friends,
particularly those who do not yet realise
the extent of God's love for them.

Silence

Christ is the image:
of the invisible God we worship.

May those who have been scattered
far from their homes and loved ones
be enabled to live again in peace and happiness;
may the bitter and resentful find hope again
and the confused find new direction.

Silence

Christ is the image:
of the invisible God we worship.

May the dying know the closeness of God,
and those who mourn their loved ones
know for certain that God's kingdom
stretches across both sides of death.

Silence

Christ is the image:
of the invisible God we worship.

We pray with Mary,
Mother of Christ the King:
Hail, Mary . . .

In the warmth of God's love,
we pray in silence now
for our own particular concerns.

Silence

Celebrant
God our Father,
we ask you to accept our prayers,
through Christ our Lord.
Amen.

SPECIAL FEASTS
YEARS A, B, C

Mary, Mother of God
1 January

Jesus Christ, the Son of God, is born of a woman.

Celebrant
Let us still our bodies and souls
as we gather to pray to the God
who made us and loves us.

Reader
As the Church we are the Body of Christ;
we give thanks for Mary's mothering
which we share with Jesus,
and pray that her love and faithfulness
will inspire in us a spirit of willing co-operation.

Silence

Your will, Lord:
be done in us.

Out of love for the world
God sent his Son into the world;
we pray for all who live in the darkness of sin,
for the places where evil and corruption flourish,
where the problems and troubles
seem almost too entrenched to be solved.
We pray for hearts to be healed of hatred
and hope to be rekindled.

Silence

Your will, Lord:
be done in us.

As we remember with gratitude
Mary's mothering in the home at Nazareth,
we pray for our own homes and families,
for all expectant mothers,
those giving birth and the children being born,

that they may be surrounded and upheld
with love and affection.

Silence

Your will, Lord:
be done in us.

As we call to mind those we know
who are in trouble, need or sorrow,
we pray for comfort and healing,
refreshment and encouragement.

Silence

Your will, Lord:
be done in us.

We give thanks that through the cross
death no longer has the victory;
we pray for those mothers who have died to this life
that they may know the fullness of joy in heaven.

Silence

Your will, Lord:
be done in us.

We pray with Mary,
our spiritual mother:
Hail, Mary . . .

Meeting our heavenly Father
in the stillness of silence,
let us whisper to him
our particular burdens of prayer.

Silence

Celebrant
Father, we bring these prayers
through Jesus Christ, our Saviour.
Amen.

THE PRESENTATION OF THE LORD (CANDLEMAS) – 2 FEBRUARY

In accordance with Jewish tradition,
the Light of the World is presented as a first-born baby
in the temple at Jerusalem.

Celebrant
As we gather in Christ's name,
let us bring to mind those
who particularly need our prayer support.

Reader
We remember those who teach the faith
throughout the Church and throughout the world.
May the Lord keep them close to his guiding,
and open the hearts of those they teach
to hear and receive his truth.

Silence

Show us your ways:
and help us to walk in them.

We remember those in positions
of authority and influence
in this country and in all societies,
that needs may be noticed and addressed,
good values upheld and all people respected.

Silence

Show us your ways:
and help us to walk in them.

We remember those who looked after us
when we were very young,
and those who have no one to love and care for them.
We remember all young families
and all the children in our parish,
that they may be introduced to the one true God
and live their lives in his company.

Silence

Show us your ways:
and help us to walk in them.

We remember the elderly faithful
and especially those who are housebound
and can no longer join us to worship in person.
We give thanks for their example
and pray for an increase of our love for one another
across the age groups.

Silence

Show us your ways:
and help us to walk in them.

We remember those who have finished
their lives on earth
and commit them to the Father's everlasting care
and protection.
We ask him to keep us faithful to the end of our life.

Silence

Show us your ways:
and help us to walk in them.

We offer our prayers with Mary
who took on the joys and sorrows
of mothering Jesus:
Hail, Mary . . .

In silence, let us bring to our God
the concerns of our own hearts,
knowing his love for us all.

Silence

Celebrant
Father, through the light of life
we are enabled to pray,
in the assurance of your faithfulness.
We offer our prayers
through Christ, the Light of the World.
Amen.

SAINT JOHN THE BAPTIST – 24 JUNE

*John is born with a mission to prepare the way
for the Messiah by calling people to repentance.*

Celebrant
Let us pray together in the presence of God.

Reader
Into every situation of doubt
and despondency among his followers
may the Father breathe his faithfulness.

Silence

Prepare us, O Lord:
to walk in your ways.

Into our strongholds of ambition
and defensiveness
may the Father breathe his humility.

Silence

Prepare us, O Lord:
to walk in your ways.

Into the prisons of guilt and revenge
may the Father breathe the grace of his forgiveness.

Silence

Prepare us, O Lord:
to walk in your ways.

Into the darkness of pain and fear
may the Father breathe his reassurance.

Silence

Prepare us, O Lord:
to walk in your ways.

Into our complacency
may the Father breathe his zeal.

Silence

Prepare us, O Lord:
to walk in your ways.

Into our homes and places of work
may the Father breathe his fellowship and love.

Silence

Prepare us, O Lord:
to walk in your ways.

Into the whole of his creation
may the Father breathe his joy and peace.

Silence

Prepare us, O Lord:
to walk in your ways.

We make our prayer with Mary,
who rejoiced with her cousin Elizabeth
over the birth of John the Baptist:
Hail, Mary . . .

In silence, let us bring our private prayers
to the loving mercy of God.

Silence

Celebrant
Father, like John the Baptist,
may we courageously prepare the way
for the coming of the kingdom.
Through Christ, our Lord.
Amen.

SAINTS PETER AND PAUL – 29 JUNE

*Through the dedication of the apostles Peter and Paul, the Gospel
of Jesus Christ spread and the Church was rapidly established.*

Celebrant
Gathered as the Church of God,
let us pray.

Reader
As we celebrate the life and work of Peter and Paul,
we give thanks for our Church
and its faithfulness through the ages.
We ask the Lord to bless the Pope
and all leaders, pastors and teachers in the Church,
that they may be always open and attentive
to his guiding Spirit.

Silence

In all things, Father:
may your will be done.

As we recall the opposition and persecution
experienced by Peter and Paul,
we pray for all who are persecuted and threatened
for their faith today,
and for those working to discredit and crush
the influence of the Church.
We pray for the leaders of the nations
and those who advise and support them,
that they may seek what is right and good,
and bear in mind the needs of those they serve.

Silence

In all things, Father:
may your will be done.

We pray that in our daily prayers and conversations,
our daily work and service,
we may remain true to Christ's teaching
and love with his compassion,
whatever the cost.

Silence

In all things, Father:
may your will be done.

We pray for all who are imprisoned,
whether physically, emotionally or spiritually;
May the Lord free them to live in the freshness of his love
and the security of his faithfulness.

Silence

In all things, Father:
may your will be done.

As we recall with gratitude the willingness of Peter and Paul
to risk their lives in the Lord's service,
we pray for all who have died in faith
and thank the Lord for their love and commitment.
May he welcome them into his eternity;
may they know his peace and joy for ever.

Silence

In all things, Father:
may your will be done.

We join our prayers
with those of Mary our Mother:
Hail, Mary . . .

In the stillness of God's peace,
we bring our personal prayers
to our loving Father.

Silence

Celebrant
Father, accept these prayers
for the Church and for the world;
we pray that in all things
your kingdom may come.
Through Jesus Christ our Lord.
Amen.

THE TRANSFIGURATION OF THE LORD – 6 AUGUST

*Jesus is seen in all God's glory,
and as fulfilling the Law and the prophets.*

Celebrant
Let us quieten ourselves
in the presence of the living God,
as we pray.

Reader
The Father knows us better than we know ourselves,
and is well aware of the needs and pains
in his Church.
We lift them now to his healing love.

Silence

Father, we love you:
open our eyes to see your glory.

In our world there are decisions to be made,
countries to be governed and people to be honoured.
We lift them now to his grace and wisdom.

Silence

Father, we love you:
open our eyes to see your glory.

In our neighbourhood and in our homes
there are celebrations and tragedies,
times of hope, weariness and tenderness.
We lift them now to his parenting.

Silence

Father, we love you:
open our eyes to see your glory.

In our hospitals and clinics there are many in pain,
many who are fearful,
and many who have lost hope.
We lift them now to his comfort and protection.

Silence

Father, we love you:
open our eyes to see your glory.

As each day others die and enter God's presence,
we ask his mercy
and commend them to his safekeeping.

Silence

Father, we love you:
open our eyes to see your glory.

We pray with Mary
who saw in her Son the glory of God:
Hail, Mary . . .

Let us be still and silent in God's presence
and pray in faith to our loving Father.

Silence

Celebrant
Father, as the disciples saw your glory
revealed in Jesus,
so may your glory be revealed in us.
Through Christ our Lord.
Amen.

THE ASSUMPTION – 15 AUGUST

The Almighty has done great things for me!

Celebrant
As children of our heavenly Father,
let us gather ourselves to pray.

Reader
On this feast of the Assumption,
we give thanks for the mothering love of Mary,
Mother of Christ and his Body, the Church.
We pray for each member of the Church of God,
both lay and ordained,
in their ministry to encourage one another
as loving servants to the needs of the world.

Silence

Lord of life:
may your kingdom come.

We pray for the world Christ died to save,
with its diversity of cultures and beliefs,
expectations and memories,
and its shared resources and human needs;
we pray for those who lead and govern,
for responsible stewardship
and wise decision-making.

Silence

Lord of life:
may your kingdom come.

We pray for our parents and our own families,
for all those we love and all who love us;
we pray for our friends and neighbours,
our colleagues, employers and employees;
we pray for those on either side of us now.

Silence

Lord of life:
may your kingdom come.

We pray for those who are in pain,
sorrow or distress,
that they may know God's presence
and receive his comfort and healing.

Silence

Lord of life:
may your kingdom come.

We pray for those who have died
and all who grieve for them;
we pray for those dying alone and unnoticed,
we pray for those dying unwanted and unborn.

Silence

Lord of life:
may your kingdom come.

We pray with Mary,
our Mother in heaven:
Hail, Mary . . .

In the silence of eternity,
let us bring to our loving Father
the concerns of our own hearts.

Silence

Celebrant
Father, with Mary we know
that you give us abundant blessing;
hear these prayers in mercy and love.
Through Christ our Lord.
Amen.

THE TRIUMPH OF THE HOLY CROSS
14 SEPTEMBER

Through Christ's loving obedience,
even to death on a cross, he has opened up
the way for us to eternal life.

Celebrant
In the knowledge of the extent of God's love for us,
let us pray.

Reader
We pray for all in the Church
whose journey through life is hard,
dangerous, exhausting or confused.

Silence

Lord of love:
you have won the victory.

We pray for those whose lives
are disrupted, oppressed or devastated
by war, famine or political unrest.

Silence

Lord of love:
you have won the victory.

We pray for our families, friends and neighbours;
all who cause us concern
and all in need of peace.

Silence

Lord of love:
you have won the victory.

We pray for those whose lives
are filled with pain, resentment or hatred;
for all who are trapped in addiction or despair.

Silence

Lord of love:
you have won the victory.

We pray for those who have died
and for those who miss them;
we thank the Lord for saving us through the cross
so that we can hope to share the glory of heaven.

Silence

Lord of love:
you have won the victory.

We join our prayers with those of Mary,
who witnessed the tragedy
and the triumph of the cross:
Hail, Mary . . .

As we kneel at the foot of the cross,
trusting in its power to save,
let us bring to the Lord our own prayers.

Silence

Celebrant
Father, you gave us the gift of your Son;
accept these prayers and transform our lives.
Through Christ our Lord.
Amen.

ALL SAINTS – 1 NOVEMBER

Lives that have shone with God's love on earth
are filled with joy as they see their Lord face to face.

Celebrant
Knowing our dependence on God in all things,
let us pray to him now.

Reader
As we celebrate the lives of those Church members
who have shone with the brightness of love,
we ask that the Lord may refresh our commitment
and conscious awareness of our need for him
in this parish and as individual Christians.

Silence

Just as I am:
I come.

May the kingdom of love and peace
be established in this world and grow.
We pray for both the influential and the ignored,
both the popular and the disliked,
both the ambitious and the vulnerable.
May the Lord teach us all his ways and his values.

Silence

Just as I am:
I come.

We call to mind our families and friends,
neighbours and colleagues,
giving thanks for all the loving care and forgiveness
the Lord has shown them,
and we ask him to shine his light
in all areas of hurt and misunderstanding.

Silence

Just as I am:
I come.

We bring to the God of healing
those whose lives are darkened by pain, fear or weariness.

May he come to our aid, help us to bear what must be carried,
and take from us all resentment and bitterness,
replacing it with the abundance of peace.

Silence

Just as I am:
I come.

We thank the eternal God for all the saints –
those recognised by the Church
and those known only to a few, and to him.
We rejoice that they live in heaven
with every tear wiped away.
May all who have died in the friendship of the Lord
know his mercy and lasting peace.

Silence

Just as I am:
I come.

May the gracious God take us as we are
and transform us by his life in us.
May he clear our lives of all that is not of him,
so that we let his goodness shine through the colours
of our personalities and gifts he has given us.

Silence

Just as I am:
I come.

We join our prayers with those of Mary
and all the saints:
Hail, Mary . . .

In a time of silence
and in the presence of all the saints in heaven,
let us pray for our particular concerns.

Silence

Celebrant
Father, as we celebrate the joy of those
whose wills are united with yours,
we commend to you our lives
and our hope of heaven,
through Christ our Lord.
Amen.

Feasts of the Dedication of a Church

The church building symbolises the spiritual temple,
being built of the living stones of God's people.

Celebrant
Gathered as the Church of Christ in this place,
let us pray together in his name.

Reader
We give thanks for this church building
and the privilege of worshipping without fear.
We give thanks for all
who have prayed and ministered here,
and ask that the Lord will keep us attentive to his voice,
worshipping him in spirit and in truth.

Silence

Take us, Lord:
renew us and use us.

We pray for this area and its problems,
for all who live, work and raise their families here.
We give thanks for all that is good and hopeful,
and ask the Lord to bless and guide those in authority.

Silence

Take us, Lord:
renew us and use us.

May the homes we represent and all the homes of this parish
be filled with light and love,
warmth and welcome,
comfort and peace.

Silence

Take us, Lord:
renew us and use us.

May all who come to this place
in distress of body or soul
find here healing and refreshment,
and be touched with the beauty of God's holiness.

Silence

Take us, Lord:
renew us and use us.

We commend to the Father's love
all those who have worshipped here in the past,
both those we remember
and those known only to him.

Silence

Take us, Lord:
renew us and use us.

We make our prayers with Mary,
the Mother of the Church:
Hail, Mary . . .

In a time of silence, filled with God's peace,
we bring our personal prayers and petitions,
in the assurance of God's love.

Silence

Celebrant
Father, hear these prayers
which we offer as your people,
and build us as living stones
into a spiritual temple.
Through Christ our Lord.
Amen.